A JOHN CATT PUBLICATION

THE SCH
BUSINESS
MANAGER'S
HANDBOOK

In Partnership with...

Hayley Dunn

ASCL Association
of School and
College Leaders

First Published 2018

by John Catt Educational Ltd,
15 Riduna Park, Station Road
Melton, Woodbridge IP12 1QT

Tel: +44 (0) 1394 389850
Email: enquiries@johncatt.com
Website: www.johncatt.com

ISBN: 978 1 909717 72 0

Set and designed by John Catt Educational Ltd

Contents

Foreword

Being a business manager is an excellent career choice. The role is challenging, inspiring and gives you the chance to be innovative and creative. What we do makes a real difference to the lives of young people, which is incredibly rewarding.

I did not write this book because I think that everyone should be like me and work in the same way, far from it. In sharing my experiences and knowledge, and that of other school business professionals, my aim is to give you the opportunity to challenge your thinking and develop your own practice. Through collaboration and networking we can support and encourage each other, and use the shared experience of overcoming challenges to help us grow and develop as professionals.

What I have done is to learn as much as possible by reading books, attending conferences, taking part in social media discussions and asking questions. I have tried new things – not all of them have worked – but when I experienced failure, I learned, and when I was successful, I shared that knowledge and experience with others. I am aware that not all business professionals are afforded this freedom. Some are not part of the senior leadership team and are not included in key decision-making meetings. Some might have delegated workloads that are unmanageable or be set expectations that are unreasonable, and not all are treated with respect and dignity. I would strongly encourage you, if you are in a situation such as this, to try using the ideas and information in this handbook. Try doing things a different way. If you know you have tried everything that you can, or it is effecting your wellbeing, change your setting before you change your profession. Every school is led differently and works in its own unique ways.

The ideas in this book are suggestions to help you focus on some important time-saving techniques and increase your impact as a school business leader. As I mentioned, not everything I tried has worked, but I was lucky to be in an environment where I was encouraged to try, where failure was seen as an opportunity to revise and refine learning, and where success and improvement was celebrated. As a business manager who asks a lot of questions, never be afraid to ask for help. We should each strive to be the best versions of ourselves and should celebrate the unique skills and experiences that make us special and valuable.

There are always opportunities and there is always a way forward, and it is our job to find that way. There is no doubt in my mind that business managers are unsung heroes, but from a personal perspective I am not driven by recognition, I just want to do a job that makes a difference.

> *We need to change the story we tell about our profession – to the world and to ourselves.*

Geoff Barton

Geoff was talking about the teaching profession, and I think the same can be said for school business leaders. We need to inspire the next generation of business leaders by demonstrating impact, showing confidence, developing innovative practice and embracing creative thinking. We need to take collective responsibility for our profession, replacing 'We have always done it this way' with 'How could it be done differently?', 'How could it be done better?', 'How can we be better?' and 'How can I be better?'

I hope this book inspires you to share your ideas, develop your own role, and encourage and support others in making school business management and leadership a career of choice.

Be the change.

Hayley Dunn,
April 2018

Acknowledgements

Thank you to my collaborators who have made this book a reality:

Thank you to my husband James, my two beautiful strong-minded daughters, Emily and Sophie, and all my family and friends. Your patience, love, support and encouragement always means so much to me, especially whilst I was writing the book.

John Catt Publishers – thank you for understanding the need for a book for school business professionals and for your support with this project.

ASCL – thank you to Val Andrew for the support you have given me, and for the dedicated way in which you support and champion the school business profession. You are one of my 'sheros'. Thank you to Geoff Barton and Kcarrie Valentine for making this book happen.

The team at Windmill Primary School – thank you for being an amazing team, you work in challenging circumstances and are giving children opportunities and experiences which will enable them to have great futures. You were a huge part of making me in to the business leader that I am, and I will never forget it.

And most importantly thank you to all the school business professionals who shared their experience, ideas and wisdom and gave their time to write contributions for this book:

Dawn Boyes, Cheryl Campbell, Sarah-Jane Case, Maggie Duncan, Emma Gray, Louise Hatswell, Andy Heron, Graeme Hornsby, Sarah Jones, Jo Marchant, Nickii Messer, Peter Neale, Justin Smith, Sian Turner, Sarah Walters, @WorkingSBM2017.

Business Leadership

Success is not about the background you're from, it's about the confidence you have and the effort you are willing to invest.

Michelle Obama

If I had the time ...

I posed a question on social media to school business leaders in preparation for a presentation: 'If you had one free week to spend on anything you wanted that would make a difference to pupils, what would you do with it?'

The responses were varied:

'Building relationships with local businesses. Visiting them and talking to them. Telling them about my school, its students and facilities. Hearing about what they do. Discussing how we can work together for mutual benefit.'

'Income generation and getting the local community involved and invested in the school.

Looking at everything that we do, from catering to procurement processes.'

'Leading the whole school with creative displays that present one theme in all areas of schools, including catering.'

'Summer school provision as the holidays are a difficult time for some pupils. Devising a creative Planning, Preparation and Assessment (PPA) provision for pupils.'

'Translating the curriculum via music, art, and PE for those who cannot cope academically.'

'Setting up a resource bank of class materials *ie* displays, games and masks. These are repeated annually but the resources are thrown away!'

In summary, the responses were focused on a few key areas:

- Building relationships with businesses
- Reviewing every process
- Devising creative solutions
- Creating banks of resources
- Developing the school provision
- Income generation
- Forging and strengthening links with the local community

What would you focus on? I would spend the time on income generation, starting with drafting a short, medium and long term strategy that identifies areas for investment and links with school improvement priorities and providing better outcomes for pupils. I would spend time working up costed plans and looking at available grants to see if any of the project outcomes align with the criteria.

Why do we not spend the time focused on these areas? For many school business professionals there is not the capacity to focus on these areas, they become the 'nice to do if we ever have time' tasks. So much of the way that we work in schools is reactive and that is often because of the demands of others, rather that because we are not planning and organising our time well.

The value of time

The value of our time is hard to communicate to people without us seeming pompous or full of self-importance. I try to explain it by way of chargeable time. When I worked for an accountancy company in my twenties I had to record my time in six-minute units and as much as possible had to be allocated as chargeable to clients. The company was brilliant to work for, with a firm but fair attitude, but the bottom line was always that time equates to money. Any time that was not chargeable was not adding to the profit of the company and the returns of the shareholders. We are the sum of our experiences and that mindset of chargeable time and adding value has stayed with me.

Many business managers are star players in their teams, even though most would never admit it. It can often be the case that others become over-reliant on their can-do, get-done attitude, and I think this is a mistake, you should not overload your best people, just because you know they will perform.

Transitioning

Moving between job roles is a period of transition for both us as the new business manager and the school or multi-academy trust (MAT) that we go to work for, largely because there is not a stereotypical school business professional. We come from all sorts of backgrounds including finance, accountancy, human resources (HR), marketing, public relations (PR), local authority and the commercial sector, but what we all have in common is that we bring to our new positions a set of transferable skills and experiences. I do not believe that there are many who have planned for a career in school business management, although I hope this is changing and that there will be future generations actively seeking a career in school business leadership.

I came to be a school business manager (SBM) through a succession of events and opportunities. After working in a private sector accountancy company I decided that I wanted public sector accounting experience to broaden my understanding and knowledge. I got a position as a finance officer at a local authority, then an opportunity came up on the schools' finance team and it was decided that I had the accountancy experience to take on the role. I was given a caseload of schools and soon found that the most enjoyable part of the job was working with headteachers and business managers on their budget planning and monitoring. This experience gave me the opportunity to visit a range of school settings and made me aware of the SBM role, it also made me aware that this was a possible future career move.

Looking back, I wish that I had found my peer networks earlier because I have learned so much from others. It can be incredibly hard to get to grips with the role if you are not given a full induction, including things that may seem obvious, such as what needs doing, where things are, or a list of contact details. Clear initial guidance on such things can make a huge difference. When I first started in post, there must have been lots of things that I should have been doing, but that I wasn't aware of, and this is before you start on the little bits of detail that you pick up along the way. For example, who tells you that if you have a minibus you need a Section 19 permit, which is renewed every five years? Something I try to do now is build files, whether paper or electronic, that another member of staff could pick up and understand, making things as easy as possible to follow.

MAT

Moving from a maintained single school to a multi-academy trust has been an interesting transition. Appointing an audit firm who do termly visits, along with the usual year-end audit work has been a brilliant source of support in ensuring that the statutory responsibilities are discharged properly.

View from an expert

Titles – Val Andrew, ex-ASCL Business Leadership Specialist

This is a profession that has acquired a range of titles over time. Once referred to as the Bursar (originally derived from the Latin word *bursa* meaning purse) which was prevalent in the independent school sector, the title of school business manager evolved as a direct result of the workforce reform initiative implemented when Estelle Morris was Secretary of State for Education in 2001. Subsequent government initiatives have led to the appearance of several alternative titles including a some generic expressions – school business leader and school business professional. You may also encounter the CFO – chief financial officer, the COO – chief operating officer and a range of roles expressed as 'director of … ' which may express their remit for support services, financial services, estates management, and so forth.

The emergence of growing groups of schools as multi-academy trusts (MATs) or federations will give rise to and perpetuate another range of titles, perhaps referencing such roles as contracts management, marketing and brand management, and procurement. It does not matter what it says on someone's badge, what matters is the range of their roles and responsibilities, and how well they perform them.

Throughout this book you will see references to many different titles, all of which are relevant in terms of school business leadership.

Ethics and principles

Success is liking yourself, liking what you do, and liking how you do it.

Maya Angelou

Being ethical and moral, with strong principles of knowing what is right and what is wrong, is a fundamental part of my personality. I was brought up in a family where honesty, integrity and being a good, kind person, were non-negotiable expectations. There are high expectations set for the way that we conduct ourselves and rightly so, we have responsibility not only for the learning and development of the young people who are the future, but also millions of pounds of public money. We are all role models.

As an individual working within the public sector we must abide by the Nolan Principles and as members of professional bodies and through undertaking qualifications, we subscribe to these expectations in everything we do.

The Nolan Principles

The Nolan Principles are the Seven Principles of Public Life. They apply to anyone who works as a public office holder and were first set out by Lord Nolan in 1995.

The seven principles are:

- Selflessness
- Integrity
- Objectivity
- Accountability
- Openness
- Honesty
- Leadership

When I completed the ACCA qualification, it was reinforced that being a member meant abiding by the following five fundamental ethical principles, as set out in their rulebook:

- Integrity – being straightforward and honest in all professional and business relationships.
- Objectivity – not allowing bias, conflicts of interest or undue influence of others to override professional or business judgements.
- Professional competence and due care – to maintain professional knowledge and skill at a level required to ensure that a client or employer receives competent professional service based on current developments in practice, legislation and techniques, and act diligently and in accordance with applicable technical and professional standards.
- Confidentiality – to respect the confidentiality of information acquired as a result of professional and business relationships and, therefore, not disclose any such information to third parties without proper and specific authority, unless there is a legal or professional right or duty to disclose, nor use the information for the personal advantage of the professional accountant or third parties.
- Professional behaviour – to comply with relevant laws and regulations and avoid any action that discredits the profession.

Behaviours

Accepted behaviours come from the top down. It is important to me that I always treat people how I want to be treated myself, and that I demonstrate positive leadership behaviours. I try to take ownership and build trust that is underpinned by honesty and integrity.

We all start somewhere, and it is important to empower others by giving them what they need to succeed, through the provision of support, encouragement, guidance, challenge and the right level of stretch. Getting the balance of these elements right is part of good leadership. For instance a lack of challenge can lead to people becoming bored, disinterested and demotivated, while too much challenge with not enough support can mean they feel overloaded, stressed and demotivated.

Below are the positive leadership behaviours, as outlined in the National Professional Qualifications:

- Commitment – to pupils, and to improving their social mobility, wellbeing and productivity.
- Collaboration – with a range of partners.
- Personal drive – self motivation and a creative problem solving approach.
- Resilience – to remain courageous and be positive in challenging circumstances.
- Awareness – know yourself and your team, be reflective.
- Integrity – honesty, transparency and acting always in the interests of the school and pupils.
- Respect – for the rights, views, beliefs and faiths of pupils, colleagues and stakeholders.

As a member of the Institute of School Business Leaders (ISBL), I represent the profession and the Institute, so it is vital that the following behaviours are demonstrated and that at all times I should be a:

- change catalyst – curious and experimental, with the determination to methodically apply a vision of what will make a difference to the school or trust.
- decision maker – who understands and analyses data and information to identify options, make recommendations and deliver evidence-based and timely decisions.
- skilled negotiator – with the ability to work across diverse stakeholder groups and influence decisions to ensure engagement and support to achieve the aims and objectives of the school or trust.
- collaborative operator – who works inclusively and effectively with both internal and external stakeholders.

- resilient personality – who shows an ability to use existing resources to overcome challenges and creates new and effective solutions in the face of adversity.

- challenger – who demonstrates courage, emotional intelligence, integrity and the confidence to challenge others even if met with resistance.

If you are a member of any professional body, such as ICAEW, RICS, CIPFA, CIMA, or CIPD, you will be aware of something similar. The content of these various sets of principles is broadly similar; being honest and behaving with integrity, having the ability to change things that we see as being wrong, and not being afraid to shy away if that conversation is difficult. When I come up against resistance to a suggestion for an improvement, I ask myself why I am making the recommendation. I am not doing it to be awkward, or to increase anyone's workload. It is because with the benefit my knowledge and experience I can see that something can be better; that it will reduce a risk, or save time, or save money. It can be irritating, feeling that you need to justify yourself and your decisions, but remember that not everyone has the experience or knowledge that you do.

Resilience is something that is essential for a business professional, if you are met with adversity then you must have the ability to pick yourself up and come back the next day smiling. There are elements of the role that are extremely challenging, such as trying to do more with less, and feeling as if you are being blamed for pretty much everything, from resources not arriving on time to the photocopier breaking down. Of course, these things are not our fault, but to whom do people turn when a problem needs resolving? Many of us enjoy and thrive on the way that no two days are the same and the variety of the role. We love the way that we get to use our planning and problem solving skills, but every so often it would be great to be able work for an hour without being interrupted. Just like the headteacher, we love it when someone comes to us with a solution, not just a problem and an expectation that we will drop everything to sort it out.

One of the best pieces of advice I have heard about working in the education sector is 'Change your context before you change your profession' and the second which is more specifically above leadership, is 'Be an outward facing leader'.

Leadership

Leadership is about making others better as a result of your presence and making sure that impact lasts in your absence.

Sheryl Sandberg

First and foremost, enjoy the role and accept early on that you will never get everything done. Do not pretend to be something that you are not, or that you are coping when you are not. Understand your role; establish what is important and what is not. The school business leader role is varied and complex, and you will have to prioritise carefully. Sometimes that decision will be taken out of your hands, as you deal with a pressing issue, but do not let this become the norm.

Work hard and lead by example. That does not mean working 24 hours a day, seven days a week, but rather show the qualities and work ethic of a leader that you would want to follow. Carve out your own path and be who you are.

Build networks and professional relationships. Whether you are new in post or looking to move your existing organisation forward, having people around you that challenge your thinking, suggest solutions and provide encouragement is always useful. A balance of challenge and support will help us to make progress.

View from an expert

Leadership – Nickii Messer, school business management and leadership consultant; operational lead Anglia Ruskin University ILM SBM diploma programmes

Being a school business leader requires considerable imagination, drive, motivation and salesmanship. It is not enough to have the big, brave ideas, you also need the determination, the grit, and the energy to make them happen. And that means getting staff on board.

Leadership is all about courage, the courage that comes from the very core of the word; *coeur*, the French word for heart. To absolutely know, down to your very heart, that what you want to do is necessary to improve the life chances and wellbeing of the children, and that it is bound up in the values of the school.

To be a successful leader, you will need credibility. You need to be able to confidently walk the walk and talk the talk every day.

The school business leader should be a member of the senior leadership team, and this is where your credibility, and often your mettle, will truly be measured. You need to be able to assume equal status with your SLT colleagues, whatever they may feel about that to be able to pose pertinent and probing questions. You need to immerse yourself in every aspect of every meeting, don't ever allow yourself to be fobbed off by that old chestnut 'You don't need to come to this meeting, we are only talking about teaching and learning.' Well that is exactly what your job is all about. Always take your fair share of duties and only ever do your fair share of making the coffee.

The litmus test is this. If reading this doesn't excite you. If it doesn't get your juices going. Well, perhaps you're just not cut out to be type of leader that your school really truly needs and deserves.

Deepen your understanding

Solve problems, make art, think deeply.

Susan Cain

One of my most valuable experiences working within education came from attending a Year 6 residential outdoor learning trip to Wales. This was because I could clearly see the value of what I was doing, in other words, it strengthened my 'Why'. Why I was working in this type of school, why I was working in this community, why what we as a team did was so important.

The experience with 40 children, many from disadvantaged backgrounds, was humbling; observing them being away from home – many for the first time – seeing them experience new things, watching them push themselves to overcome fears of water or heights.

An unforgettable moment was watching a boy in my group see the sea for the first time. He was mesmerised by it, he walked to the edge and sat down in the shallows enjoying the sensation of the water. The school had made this possible, making the arrangements, sorting the finances, filling out risk assessments, staff taking time away from their homes and families to make it happen; and the boy went home having had a wonderful life experience, that he will hopefully never forget.

Purpose

I have always had a strong sense of purpose and wanting to help others. The experience of looking at things from the children's point of view and seeing the impact that our actions have for them reinforced for me why having a purpose and doing things to make a difference is so important; it really helps to get you through those tough days.

Make sure that you take some time to understand teaching and learning in your school; go in to classes, meetings, parent events, assemblies and trips or visits. You need to fully understand and appreciate the context, challenges and opportunities of the children and adults you work with if you are going to add value or save money. Know your stakeholders and be a leader who is visible and accessible.

This methodology is endorsed by Drew Povey in 'Educating Drew' and by Mary Myatt in 'High Challenge, Low Threat'. They both highlight the use of 'management by wandering around', a theory that was developed at Hewlett-Packard in 1970's, which encourages us to notice everything. I know that there have been times that I have worried about things at work which were outside of my control and that I could not influence or change. I now try to put these things to one side (this is not always easy) and focus on what I can do. Focus on what you can control.

Introversion

> *The secret to life is to put yourself in the right lighting. For some it's a Broadway spotlight; for others, a lamp lit desk. Use your natural powers – of persistence, concentration, insight, and sensitivity – to do work you love and work that matters.*

Susan Cain

I am an Introvert, and my Myers Briggs personality type is ISTJ. ISTJs are the 'Logistician', we are logical, organised, sensible and strong traditionalists, who enjoy keeping our work, lives and environments well-regulated. We are known as being quiet, responsible and reliable. Perseverance is a strength and we form the backbone of the organisations we work for, with a strong belief in commitment and loyalty.

Introverts can be brimming with ideas, thoughts and views and are often just waiting for the extroverts to stop talking so they can find the right moment to speak up. As a leader, I believe in going around the table in meetings and asking each person what their view is. If you have an introvert in your team it is likely that they have a lot more to offer than what they add if left unprompted. Find a way to encourage these people to speak up.

Appreciate each individual's qualities and play to their strengths. Using emotional intelligence or profiling techniques can help you in understanding each of your team members. The greatest leaders are not always the loudest, I assure you that quiet people can have the loudest minds.

Greatness

The greatest business leaders I have met are adaptable and flexible in meeting conflicting, demanding needs. They are proactive in nature, resourceful, innovative, and forward thinking in their practice. They encourage themselves and others to improve and succeed, empower multi-discipline teams and support continual professional development that meets individual and organisational needs. They are agile forward thinking leaders, demonstrated by their level of understanding and communication and their commitment to collaboration.

They are resilient and tenacious, and they focus on getting the important things done.

View from an expert

Agility – Val Andrew, ASCL business leadership specialist

School business leaders need various skills and competencies in order to be effective, but above all they need to be agile. I realise that 'agility' appears to have become a buzzword in the professional world but humour me briefly.

The dictionary describes 'agile' as 'Able to move quickly and easily … Able to think and understand quickly.' Other relevant adjectives include nimble, alert, sharp, clever, shrewd, perceptive and astute. I challenge any current practitioner to dispute that these are the qualities we possess in abundance – along with a plethora of others.

While the traditional role of a generalist bursar has been around for over 100 years based on the independent sector model, the role of school business manager within state schools has only emerged relatively recently since the implementation of the Local Management of Schools programme (LMS) in 1988. Despite a rapid rise in popularity the role continues its evolutionary journey and now manifests itself in a number of guises. There are generalist roles with a wide all-encompassing remit, specialist roles focusing on discrete aspects of business functionality like financial management, HR management or estates management, and there are executive roles often badged as Chief Operating Officer (COO) that draw on the characteristics of similar roles in the private sector. There is without doubt great diversity within the school business profession.

We have shared challenges with our leadership colleagues; the expectation that we can deliver consistency, keep student attainment on an upward trajectory, manage constant change, keep staff motivated in an uncertain climate, successfully manage pressured budgets, deliver innovation and squeeze every last drop of efficiency from our resources. And doing all this with a smile on our face and with a skin thick enough to combat a barrage of criticism which can manifest itself from anywhere, even from within our own organisations. Many practitioners report internal resistance to the concept of a 'non-teacher' knowing anything relevant about education or the organisation of our institutions. I have kicked back against the use of that term for many years and disappointingly it still features in some areas of the sector including Department for Education reports. Where else in this world are professionals described by what they don't do? I could also be described as a 'non-astronaut' or a 'non-brain surgeon' .

Back to agility – the fractured educational landscape that we navigate on a daily basis is constantly changing and as leaders within that environment we need to be able to deliver consistency and be adaptable in order to succeed.

A = adaptable and authentic

G = grit (and determination), granular and have gravitas

I = innovative and intuitive

L = legitimacy and lead (be the leader you would follow)

E = ethical and emotionally intelligent

This book is going to be an invaluable resource for practitioners as they move through our education system as credible and agile leaders who bring an additional and alternative dimension to the leadership function. It is no longer just about saving a percentage of the headteacher's time – which is an outdated concept – there are vital business activities that educational organisations have to deliver, and school business leaders are the people with that responsibility, a responsibility which ultimately impacts on the experiences of the children and young people within the system.

View from an expert

The context for effective school business management – Graeme Hornsby, SBM Consultancy Ltd

An overview of some of the key features of the context in which schools are operating along with considerations and implications for school business leaders.

School partnerships look here to stay

The most effective leaders I see are in touch with the evolving context of the school system and prepare themselves and position their organisations accordingly. We have seen this most recently with the emergence of partnerships either formally with multi-academy trusts or through strong collaborations. While some see this as protection from being forced into particular courses of action or partnerships not of their choosing, many are reaping real rewards from more proactive partnership working. Guidance from ASCL in the 2016 report 'Staying in Control of Your School's Destiny' provides useful information in this area and Robert Hill's 2015 blog provides a helpful view on the potential and pitfalls of academy chains.

Implications from the broadening of accountability and powers for intervention

The update in February 2018 of the Department for Education guidance on 'Schools Causing Concern' seems to have slipped under the radar of many school leaders and trustees. The powers and expectations of local authorities and regional schools commissioners for intervention remain significant and there are clear criteria for interventions and the issuance of warning notices, which include a breakdown of the way a school is managed or governed. Evidence that governors may be failing to deliver on one or more of their strategic roles could include but is not restricted to:

- high governor turnover.
- a significant unexplained change to their constitution.
- the governing body having an excessive involvement in the day-to-day running of the school.
- a lack of appropriate engagement with data, this might include,

but is not limited to, data on pupil learning and progress or staff recruitment.

- not sufficiently managing risks associated with strategic priorities and school improvement plans.
- evidence of poor financial management and oversight, such as consistent overspending the school's budget beyond agreed thresholds.

Several commentators have signalled that the next round of school partnerships is likely to be focused on financial and governance matters rather than solely or mainly on school improvement issues, and while we will need to see how powers of intervention are exercised the broadening of this guidance along with ongoing financial pressure on school budgets seems to support this view. It is not unimaginable to see the potential joining of this sharper financial accountability framework with the emergence of school efficiency advisor roles to provide support and the requirement for academy trusts to submit three-year budget forecasts which should – in theory at least – provide an earlier warning of potential issues. As for local authority schools, I see similar variations in their challenges and in capacity and capability at both school and local authority level.

The scope of business management is broadening – and narrowing

The traditional role of the school business manager with a remit including finance, HR, administration and facilities management continues to be appropriate in many settings. Some roles have narrowed into specialist roles with single or more focused areas of responsibility, with others emerging into broader remits such as chief operations officers. There are also more emerging CEO roles where the 'E' is more executive and less educationalist. Whereas the mantra used to be that every school should have an effective school business manager it is now the case that every school should have effective business management.

In too many schools, governance has for too long sat outside the scope of business management, but with the increase in the accountability measures noted above and the direct and clearly stated responsibilities for CFOs in academy trusts to 'play both a technical and leadership role, including ensuring sound and appropriate financial governance and risk management arrangements are in place' (Education Funding Agency, 2014) we are seeing the emergence of what the Department for Education terms 'professional clerking' in the 2017 'Clerking Competency Framework', with an increasing number of trusts looking to develop more senior governance roles within their business management functions. The increasing demand for effective risk management is also apparent, especially in the design and application of due diligence around potential and growing partnerships.

Financial pressures – and the myths and realities of effective procurement

I often hear about the potential for partnerships to achieve savings from joint procurement, but with little substantive evidence of significant savings where there has been effective procurement in individual schools in the first place. This is not unexpected given what is often a limited scope for significant reductions from a supplier's point of view from single contracts or volumes. Perhaps we need to be better at focusing on and understanding where their overheads and margins are. More pertinent is the issue of materiality. It is unfortunately still the case that too many schools and trusts have not fully utilised the various tools and forms of analysis to help them examine how staff are deployed.

What value is the partnership adding?

Robert Hill's blog, mentioned earlier, includes ten principles which multi-academy trusts can use to judge the effectiveness of their performance systems. To these I would add a fundamental need for clarity on what value the multi-academy trust is already adding and the aims we need to add in our thinking about governance, leadership and wider staffing structures and into processes like performance management and development planning. The best partnerships are already benefitting from this, in others I see another layer of staffing, governance and bureaucracy on top of what was already there. There are also dangers around how partnerships might grow without proper consideration of the mix of what schools might need and what the partnership can realistically offer or broker. This brings us back to effective due diligence and the need for this to be both outward looking at the potential partners and inward looking on how the partnership structures can adapt to growth.

References

ASCL (2018) *Staying in Control of your School's Destiny: forming a multi-academy trust.* [online] Available at: www.ascl.org.uk/help-and-advice/guidance-papers/ staying-in-control-of-your-schools-destiny-forming-a-multiacademy-trust.html [Accessed 10 Apr. 2018].

Department for Education (2017) Clerking Competency Framework. London: The Stationery Office.

Department for Education (2018) *Schools Causing Concern.* London: The Stationery Office. Available at: www.gov.uk/government/publications/schools-causing-concern--2 [Accessed 10 Apr. 2018].

Education Funding Agency (2014) *Academies financial handbook 2014.* London: The Stationery Office.

Hill, R. (2015)*Academy chains.* [online] Available at: roberthilleducationblog.com/ academy-chains/ [Accessed 10 Apr. 2018].

What is it like working in the school business profession?

Being a special school business manager – Jo Marchant, AInsAM(Dip), Cert Acc, MBA, FISBL

In my opinion, the two things that you need to be successful as an SBM in a special school, in addition to the qualities required to work in a mainstream school, are thankfulness and curiosity. The thing you do not need is pity. In my school, we count ourselves fortunate to have pupils who really want to come to school every day, they even ring the school office in the holidays just to make sure that we really are closed! We do not suffer from vandalism – it simply doesn't occur to our pupils to wilfully damage their school, and some of our pupils are incredibly talented – we have a sixth former who does a brilliant performance as Elvis! Our pupils help us to keep developing ourselves as educationalists as we constantly search for new ways to engage with our unique pupil cohort.

For instance, when I read about Eye Gaze technology – an interactive screen which enables those with limited or no gross motor skills to communicate through eye movement – I passed the article on to a teacher in one of our classes for pupils with profound and multiple learning difficulties. That was three years ago, we now have three Eye Gaze systems and its use is embedded into our curriculum. I realised how significant this equipment was when I met a parent who was in tears because she'd just seen her 16-year-old daughter, who could not communicate verbally and who had no gross or fine motor control, choose something for herself using Eye Gaze for the first time. Nothing compares with making that kind of difference in a child's life, that is why I choose to work in a special school.

Pupils who are severely autistic often have difficulty in maintaining their attention span, which makes it difficult for them to focus on their learning. Our teachers have learned that short bursts of physical activity increase their attentiveness, so we have introduced a new aspect to lessons for our primary pupils which we call 'sensory circuits'. Our school is designed so that each Key Stage has its own long corridor with classrooms on either side. This gives us a long space in which pupils can use sensory equipment, such as a small trampoline, a large ball that they can flop over or squash against, and a low-level trolley which they can ride on. Pupils in each class in the Key Stage have timetabled access to this equipment and are taken out of class in groups of three. When I observed a lesson recently, I watched a pupil really struggle to focus in class, but on the trampoline she demonstrated energy and precision and was totally absorbed in that activity. When she returned to class, she was able to concentrate. Having seen the difference this equipment makes to pupils' lives means that I can understand its importance and so have no hesitation in finding funding when it is requested.

Occasionally I get the opportunity to contribute to a lesson and I am always so pleased to be asked. I make sure that I find out what the teacher is expecting of me and I prepare my lesson plan with appropriate resources in advance. When asked to talk about health and safety for example, I had the students moving around the room looking for trip hazards, I demonstrated how to lift large cardboard boxes safely, and when we talked about fire safety, I put on the hi-viz jacket that I wear during fire evacuations.

As with every school, the safeguarding of our pupils is of paramount concern and some of our pupils' behaviours mean that we really have to think about things that other schools take for granted. For example, one of our pupils has a real fixation with Christmas trees so we only put the Christmas decorations up in the dining hall one week before Christmas because once the tree is up, this pupil requires extra supervision to ensure that she doesn't pull it over. Another one of our pupils is very concerned about 'stranger danger' and gets very anxious if he meets someone in school that he does not know. Because I'm not such a familiar face to this person, when I see him I always show him my photo on my ID badge and tell him my name and who I am.

Many of our pupils experience a lot of anxiety every day and this usually starts on the journey to school with most of our pupils travelling in on minibuses and taxis provided by the local authority. Assisting 265 pupils to disembark safely in our car park every morning is a major operation. Four years ago, my school had the opportunity to extend the car park in order to facilitate a quicker flow of vehicles at the start and end of the day. Everything was ready to go on the project, but the local authority was refusing to give permission to proceed because of some minor details. We had worked hard to get the project to this point and I knew that I only had a day or two to give the go ahead to the contractors in order for it to be completed by the end of the summer holidays. I went to the local authority offices and sat in their reception until I got to see the officer in charge and then I explained just what a difference this extension would make to our pupils' lives. We got the required permission and the works went ahead as planned. I knew that all my hard work and tenacity was worth it when teachers started telling me how much calmer pupils were at the start of the day and the positive effect this was having on their ability to learn.

Being a business manager of a school and a teaching school, the weird and winding road of my SBM journey – Maggie Duncan, FISBL, school business manager, The Redeemer CEP

After finishing my degree in English language and literature, my next step was teacher training. I wanted to be like my favourite teacher who made learning fun. I was accepted onto the programme and started my first placement at a local primary school. I enjoyed the work and found it fulfilling, but also found it difficult to constantly see the enjoyment and learning of the children being superseded by the demands of SATs results and other testing. I believed that results were being put before the wellbeing of the children and decided to leave.

I got the first job that came along which was a salesperson in a holiday call centre, and then moved to a cashier's position at a local bank. I progressed to counter manager, spending a lot of time at my desk auditing and number crunching. After two years a friend showed me an advertisement for a senior finance officer at a local high school. The job description asked for all the skills I had picked up at the bank and so I applied. The interview day consisted of an interview with the headteacher and deputy, and then a task where we had to prioritise a list of jobs and reconcile a bank statement. I got to the bank statement and as the adding machine was faulty I had to improvise and show my workings manually rather than attaching the adding machine receipt.

I spent the next five years learning from the best, and most stubborn, school business manager I know. She was fanatical about detail and did her utmost to teach me everything she knew while being passionate about the children's experience at the school. She was typically seen, as we all are at some point, as the person that said 'no', but she tirelessly worked, often without acknowledgement, to generate income and find cost savings to ensure the children experienced everything they could while they were at the school.

Unfortunately, due to ill health I spent much of the next two years covering her role of school business manager (SBM). The systems and processes in place were fantastic so I concentrated on the operational aspects to keep the school running and got my first experience of attending senior leadership team (SLT) and governors' meetings. These were overwhelming at first as I wasn't sure what was expected and didn't want to let down my line manager in her absence, but I soon found my feet with the help of a great SLT. It was in these meetings that I really learned how teaching and learning, and business management come together to improve outcomes for children. I also undertook my certificate of school business management (CSBM). I really struggled with the theory but loved applying leadership and business strategies to my setting.

failure is just a growth curve,

When the long standing SBM retired the post was advertised but my application was not successful. I did not want to take a backwards step and took a position in a primary school in a nearby town. I took over from a long serving office manager which really enhanced my skills in change management. Only two months into the role I found out I was pregnant and while on maternity leave found that the school just four minutes from my house would shortly be advertising for an SBM. The school had a fantastic local reputation and was rated 'outstanding' by Ofsted, as well as being known for being a great place to work. Given that my daily commute was three hours, I applied, and have never looked back.

I was appointed as the SBM and the teaching school business manager. It really is a great place to work, the SLT is diverse which provides great balance, and the staff are hardworking. I changed a lot of things in the first two years, which is my only regret. I should have implemented new processes and procedures in a more measured fashion, which I realised after receiving feedback from one of the teaching assistants.

I'm in my fourth year at the school now, and with the help and mentorship of a great headteacher and the support of great office staff, I feel that we have done great things. I have completed my advanced diploma of school business management (ADSBM), become a fellow of the Institute of School Business Leadership, met and been inspired by many of the country's SBMs, and successfully applied for an upgrade in salary due to my SLT status. The catering manager and site manager received 'Star in our school' awards, the business team won a Pearson award, the school continues to be outstanding, is in the top 1% of the country for attainment, and this year were named primary school of the year at the local newspaper's awards ceremony.

I can honestly say it has been tough due to lack of funding, changes of legislation and all the other challenges that come with working in a school, but it is still the most satisfying job I know. Would I change it? Not for all the chocolate in the world.

If I could give one piece of advice to any current or aspiring SBMs, it would be to join a local business managers' group. I am a member of the Lancashire Association of School Business Managers and their support is invaluable.

Being a primary school business manager, #SBMLife – Cheryl Campbell, Falconbrook Primary School, Battersea, London

I first thought about becoming a school business manager many years ago, at that point I had no idea what the role entailed but thought it would be a nice move to make after several years working within the local authority. After some initial rejections I started researching in to how to make myself a suitable candidate. My first step was to collect as many job descriptions and person specifications as I could, I then identified my areas for development and set about expanding my experience. As a primary school governor, I was lucky enough to have access to a school to support me through taking my certificate in school business management (CSBM) which I took online. As someone trying to move sideways into the profession the qualification was invaluable in building my relevant knowledge.

I secured my first role before I received the notification saying I had passed my CSBM and that's when the nerves kicked in. I was worried that I didn't know enough to perform the role so I decided to make links to try and get some support. My first advice came from an established SBM in my borough, he advised me to find out about the management information system (MIS) I would be working with and see if I could familiarise myself with how it worked. Having never used an MIS before and being on a two month notice period at the local authority, I set about finding out all there was to know about the Wauton Samuel system the school used. The next piece of advice came from an old school friend who was a director of operations in a secondary school. She told me to remember that I would be in a senior management position and to behave in an appropriately authoritative manner. She let me know that I would need to be prepared to make key decisions and give well considered advice to the headteacher and governors. As someone coming from a senior position in local government I was used to making decisions and having accountability, but I still had that sinking feeling of not knowing where to start. Her final piece of advice of was to gather all the key school policies as soon as possible after taking up the position and go through them one by one to get a picture of the how the school functioned and whether or not it was compliant. Armed with this information I set about my SBM life.

As a new SBM I was lucky to have an experienced SBM from a neighbouring school to point me in the right direction. I very quickly got to grips with the finance side of the role, and having previously worked in payroll I found that aspect to be familiar and reassuringly easy. I found that I liked the satisfaction when my budget reports and reconciliations balanced perfectly every month. As a Chartered Institute of Personnel and Development (CIPD) qualified HR graduate I wasn't worried about the HR aspect of the role either, and fortunately, being in a community school meant there was always someone from Schools' HR at the end of a phone to give me guidance when I wasn't quite sure of things. I'd managed a team in the local authority so taking on an administration and premises team didn't present a challenge, and I quickly got to grips with the workings of the Wauton Samuel MIS. It is amazing to realise what you can take in your stride when given the chance.

All seemed to be going well but I had a constant sense of worry that I didn't know enough, I was worried that I didn't know what I didn't know. My solution to this was to read. I found myself seeking out books and articles on the topics I needed to know more about. I signed up to Amazon Unlimited and trawled the online library, downloading titles that could be of some use to expand my knowledge. I also joined Twitter and found a whole network of school business professionals to interact with. I had found being an SBM to be a somewhat isolated role, there is nobody else in your school doing the same thing as you, so the Twitter community turned into a great space to seek advice and share experiences. One day I posed a question about what fellow SBMs were reading, it was here that the hashtag #sbmreadinglist was born.

For me, reading is the key to developing as an SBM, I am constantly saving articles to my phone so I can read them later. I have a list as long as my arm of professional reading that I want to get around to. The topics are varied – from budgets to building maintenance, finance to fire safety, grievances to general data protection regulations (GDPR). The list goes on but there are always great books and articles out there to expand my knowledge.

I have developed a real thirst for reading and gathering knowledge, it has been essential in my development as an SBM and I cannot stress enough how important it is. The role of an SBM is so varied that it is imperative to keep abreast of all aspects and it is a role in which I will continuously learn and grow. After 26 months I still count myself as a relative newcomer to the SBM life, and although I have already learned so much there is always something new to master. My current focus is health and safety, my school is in an old Victorian building so you can imagine the health and safety implications that brings. I've recently completed an Institute of Occupational Safety and Health (IOSH) certified 'Managing Health and Safety in Education' course and am taking every opportunity to read up on how to effectively manage educational premises. I'm keen to find out what I don't know and add to my knowledge. When I'm unsure I turn to my fellow SBMs for guidance, either on Twitter or by emailing colleagues within my borough.

I plan to be in school business for a long time to come and for me the key to developing is to read, read, read and to network, network, network.

Being a trust project director, this time tomorrow … – Sian Turner, project director and clerk to Northern Schools Trust

My church does an irregular session called 'This Time Tomorrow' where members of the congregation talk in a broad sense about their work, they usually bring some props with them and we have to guess what they might do. I was pondering this recently and thinking about what I would bring in and what I would talk about if I was ever asked to appear in this slot. Walkie-talkie, clipboard, mobile phone, plunger, rubber gloves, hard hat, pen, tissues, calculator … the list goes on. That's both the beauty and frustration of life as a school business leader, the role is so varied and wide-ranging that it's hard to encompass in 100 words let alone 1,000.

I have worked in education for 20 years and my career encompasses the independent sector, maintained schools, academy schools, primary schools, secondary schools, studio schools, UTCs, boarding schools, rural, town and inner-city. Writing it down makes me realise the experience I've acquired over the years and I am grateful to all my schools for the opportunities that I've been given.

My first role was as an executive assistant to the principal of Cheltenham Ladies' College. I moved from one of the big five accountancy firms where I'd been a very successful PA and I thought 'How hard can it be?' As it turns out, it was hard, really hard. I was working one-to-one with the principal of the largest girls' boarding school in Europe, and education was a world apart from what I was used to. It wasn't the hard work – I was used to hard work – but rather the different relationships I had to build working in a school. However, I stuck it out and built an extremely good relationship with the principal – her leaving letter to me still makes me cry on those days when I doubt I have the ability to undertake the roles given to me – she believed in me and helped me develop that belief in myself.

Following a career break while I was bringing up my son, I returned to education as the school business manager of a small rural primary school. Having come from an administrative background I had asked at interview about the amount of finance involved in the role and was told it was about half a day a week. I still cannot see where that figure came from as it quickly became apparent that the finance element was the major part of the role – I had to learn quickly especially as the Financial Management Standard in Schools audit was looming. Those early days were again very hard and being in a primary school I was responsible for seemingly everything; finance, school information management systems, census, reception, and of course fishing the 'free fruit' apples out of the infants' toilets when they decided that was more fun than eating them. However, with the support of my headteacher I completed the certificate in school business management and diploma in school business management as we also became the first primary school in Herefordshire to convert to academy status.

That change was another massive learning curve and I am proud of the work we did to use our freedoms and embed the systems we wanted to improve the school experience of those pupils. We also accomplished a major building project using the academy capital improvement fund to create three brand new classrooms.

A relocation to the Northwest brought me to a multi-academy trust as a clerk to the governor's with an additional maternity cover PA role. I had forgotten how much I enjoyed the secondary phase and although moving from a small rural primary school of 180 to a large inner city secondary of 1500 was a shock, I haven't looked back.

I would be the first to say that I have been given opportunities in the last five years that I couldn't have dreamed of in a standalone school. I've worked in four of the five schools in the MAT in a substantive role and have had a substantive SLT role in one of the schools for the last 18 months. I have combined my head of governance role with other Trust-wide responsibilities including running professional development days, project management, and sitting on both the Trust operations board and the Trust-wide principals' meetings (effectively the Trust SLT). I have worked with both support and teaching colleagues who see and consider me as an integral part of the senior leadership of a school or the Trust, and I am currently being supported to acquire a further professional qualification, for which I am very grateful.

For today's school business leader the world is indeed your oyster, and regardless of school type and phase there is a rewarding and challenging career for you out there somewhere. Research what is out there, develop your networks and embrace the challenges that education continues to offer support staff. Who knows what your 'this time tomorrow' might bring.

Being a new school business manager – Sarah-Jane Case, support services manager, Mountjoy School

My interest in education began ten years ago when I volunteered as an adult helper in my daughter's class. I quickly began to appreciate the challenges and rewards of working in a school and relished any opportunity to get involved. I juggled working part time in an administrative position in adult social care and sitting on the governing body of a large primary school. The dedication and loyalty of this group of volunteers is humbling. I am very grateful to the governors I worked with as they gave me such a good grounding in school improvement and the strategies needed to plan for successful outcomes. I believe that by being a school governor, I learned many transferrable skills and techniques that support my practice now. I anticipate questions that governors may pose on my presentations and I structure my arguments around what I would want to know if I was the audience.

My first management role in education was as senior finance officer in a mainstream primary school. Although this role was finance driven, I quickly discovered that there are many cross-overs in school offices and I learned how to do a little bit of everything. After a year I moved to a leadership role within a special school. I sit on the senior leadership team and have responsibility for HR, finance and facilities. Every day is a whirlwind of meetings, e-mails and reports but I love it. I am fortunate to work with an inspirational headteacher who has a passion for personal development and all staff are supported with continued professional development (CPD). With school budgets under increasing pressure, CPD can often be an area vulnerable to cuts, but staffing is a school's most valuable resource and investment can enable the best outcomes to be delivered.

After a year at the school I enrolled on the Level 5 diploma in schools business management (DBSM), although it had been a long time since I had undertaken any formal studying. After my own time at school I completed an apprenticeship in accountancy but had never studied to a high academic standard, and I found that it takes immense discipline to work full time and complete your studies. What I found really useful about the DSBM is that it is completely relevant to my role. For example, when I had to compile a formal tender invitation for a new modular building I used the module in the course materials covering business plans, options appraisal and risk management as the basis for my report to the governors. The depth of understanding and knowledge I had gained increased the quality of my work and the whole project was much more professional as a result of my learning.

My practice is underpinned by adhering to the competencies of the school business manager framework. From conducting personal development reviews, managing disciplinary hearings, dealing with contractors or making long term financial plans, I regularly benchmark myself against those competencies to identify which areas I need to develop and apply strategies to increase my experience. As a school that is growing in pupil and staff numbers, I am frequently being exposed to new scenarios, and the most useful tool I have found for support is reaching out to other colleagues for advice. It is so interesting to hear how others have tackled a situation; what worked well and what would they do differently next time. This joint working is what encouraged me to apply for specialist leader of education status. In my application I reflected on the impact I have had on schools and the wide range of experience I have gained in many areas. I believe my interpersonal skills enable me to successfully work with other settings to help overcome the challenges they may face. I am always seeking to improve my own practice and by working and communicating with colleagues, I can see what works well for them, identify best practice and think about how I can translate that into my own and other contexts.

One of my tutors said to me that the most successful school business managers 'have the ability to read the tea leaves'. It is what is over the horizon that has the potential to impact my school, and I have taken this on board and sought to stay abreast of educational developments locally, nationally and globally. The has involved joining professional networks on social media, following governor policy, examining local government forums and contributing to consultations. I think the value school business managers can bring to schools is evidenced by the successful allocation of resources to offset the increasing challenges of the current and future economic environment.

It is so easy sometimes to forget that everyone working in schools is there for the children. School business manager roles are increasingly about the 'numbers' and the legal side of operations. To overcome this and ensure I remain focused on the fact that all of the leadership decisions I make are in the children's best interests, I do a lunch duty every week. This is such a valuable opportunity for me to see the children enjoying their lunches from the kitchen that I manage, and it also gives me an opportunity to sample the food. I can check on staffing levels, engage with staff in a different environment from my office and refresh my perspective on the suitability of facilities, resources and learning opportunities for our children.

In summary, for me to be fully effective in my role, I never stop learning. I apply the theory I have learned from the DSBM, especially in leading and managing teams. I ask for advice, and read professional journals and articles. I share my knowledge and expertise, even if it means delivering a difficult message, but this too has a positive aspect as it builds professional robustness and resilience.

My advice would be to keep up to date with educational developments and most importantly be on the side of right and keep the children at the heart of all your decisions.

Being a business manager in a multi-academy trust, a new business manager's perspective – Sarah Walters, school business manager, Shelley First School (Mast Academy Trust)

I have been a school business manager for seven months and I still have a lot to learn which, when you consider how much I have already learned in such a short time, goes some way to recognising the vast range of skills, knowledge and abilities a school business manager needs to possess.

Having worked in schools as a business support officer for three years prior to my promotion I knew that I definitely wanted to be a school business manager and that education was the sector for me. You definitely need a passion for your role and for the school you work at. I had worked for 25 years in private sector industries in roles including administrator, executive assistant and office manager, and never have I worked anywhere like the education sector. It is demanding and rewarding in equal measure which is what I believe drives me to want to succeed in my role.

I work in a small semi-rural primary school that is part of a multi-academy trust which was formed with three other schools nine months prior to me taking on my role. My work is so varied it would be hard for me to write a job description, I do have one but am sure it changes every single day! Finance forms a large part of my responsibilities as I'm sure it does for most SBMs but I am also responsible for HR, premises management, contract management, income generation, health and safety and everything in between. No two days are the same in the life of a school business manager, you can plan to have a day focusing on budgets but then find yourself dealing with a burst pipe and the day runs away with you, this though is why I love it, there is never a dull moment.

While the school was going through the academy conversion process I was also studying for my Level 4 diploma in school business management (formerly CSBM). This really helped me in my professional development and took the skills I had used in my business support position and developed them to ensure I was able to take on the role of SBM when my predecessor resigned. Completing the diploma while working full time and going through an academy conversion was tough at times but I am glad I did it, not only does the course increase your knowledge it gives you the confidence to be able to fulfil your role as a school business manager. As my final project I led on the procurement of the new financial management system for the Academy Trust. Not only did this position me to understand some of the complexities of financial reporting in academies it also allowed me to build networks with colleagues across our own Trust and also with another local Trust that was converting at around the same time.

Networks of other business managers, educational colleagues and local businesses are invaluable in your role as a school business manager, especially if you are new to the position. If you don't know the answer someone else will. When I first started I put pressure on myself to know the answer to everyone's questions which was unrealistic and unattainable. The important thing that I have learned is that it not always knowing the answers that is important, but rather knowing where to find them, and building networks is one way to achieve this.

Being part of the business management team that dealt with the initial stages of the conversion I had a good grounding in what was expected from us as we became an academy. Compliance, reporting and control responsibilities increase and it can sometimes feel like a vertical climb. I am lucky that I work closely with three very supportive business managers from the other schools in our Trust and a very patient finance director. Without them it would sometimes feel very lonely sat at my desk wondering how to tackle a certain aspect of my role. I don't think I have ever worked as hard as I have in my role as a school business manager but I am driven by my passion for the role, the school and the pupils that we teach.

I worked as part of the team developing and delivering the health and safety strategy across the Trust. Starting from scratch and writing policies, developing reporting procedures, developing compliance tracking and writing and delivering training across the Trust has not only provided me with many learning opportunities but has also built my credibility with my peers. Being part of a multi-academy trust means you have to think more like a business than ever before, thinking outside the box of education can open a whole world of opportunities for a school. This is something I want to develop in the future as I hope to make us more financially efficient, develop links with local businesses and create and develop opportunities for both my own school and the other schools within the Trust.

What advice do I wish I had been given before I took on the role? That you are only one person. As business managers we often find ourselves trying to be all things to all people. Assess the team around you, work to their strengths and empower your team to take on the responsibilities they are capable of fulfilling, this in turn will enable you to fulfil your role to the best of your ability.

Being a secondary school business manager in Wales – Andy Heron FISBL, school business manager, North Wales

Having served in the RAF for 23 years, I was aware that it is not uncommon for leavers of the forces to find that the 'real' world is somewhat different and takes some adjusting to. My second career began in August of 2006 when I started work in an English maintained 11-16 high school as a senior administrator, responsible for cover and exams. The post was a new one created in line with the updated version of the school teachers' pay and conditions document (STPCD) which detailed the administrative tasks that a teacher could no longer do.

After a short time I was coerced into becoming the finance manager (while keeping cover responsibilities of course) as the current incumbent was leaving. To say it was a steep learning curve is an understatement and unbeknown to me at the time, March was quite an important month in the school financial calendar, so I was somewhat overwhelmed with the need to ensure that the finances were in order, staff got paid and cover was apportioned and done correctly.

It became obvious to me quite early in my school career and especially after dealing with school budgets and finances that I needed to seek out some continuing professional development (CPD) that would enable me to develop my understanding and better position me within the school. With the support of the headteacher I enrolled on the certificate in school business management (CBSM) at no cost to the school except for the time away to undertake the learning I needed and successfully completed this is 2008. With my appetite for school learning whetted (and my arm twisted by a fellow recipient of the CSBM), I enrolled on the diploma in school business management (DSBM) and completed this in January 2010. Taking full advantage of the funding offered by the then National College for Teaching and Leadership (NCTL), I enrolled on the advanced diploma in school business management (ADSBM) in the spring of 2011, looking to further my career in school business management.

In my time in that English school, l had embraced the Financial Management Standards in Schools (FMSiS) and I had come to understand school funding and standards funds and the way that the local authority worked. Every year the school maintained a healthy surplus of the magical 5% and school facilities were enhanced year on year. As a cheque book school it had its advantages and although the local authority was strong in its service level agreement schemes this was a time when getting value for money and making the best deal were becoming ingrained in school life. Being progressive and business-like in arranging services and contracts was part of everyday life.

I had experienced Ofsted inspections, local authority audits, FMSiS reaccreditation and the usual trials and tribulations during my time in the school, and I knew that in order to become a school business manager I needed to move on and seek more responsibility and accountability in my role. I secured my next appointment midway through my ADSBM study and was extremely fortunate to keep the funding. Moving from an English school to a Welsh one, albeit English speaking, was on the face of it not entirely alien. The school environment was very similar where learners learned, teachers taught and support staff supported. It is obvious that nuances will be evident but, in my experience, working in English and Welsh education is in the main similar in its everyday expectations and issues.

Where it does differ significantly in my opinion and is always a cause of disagreement with political organisations is in the school funding formulas (Welsh Government, 2015). The main difference to me was the way in which the school was funded. The UK government gave the money to the Welsh Assembly and then the Welsh Assembly gave the money to the local authority. As such the figures per pupil seemed somewhat different as an element of top slicing would be taken twice; at Welsh Assembly and local authority level (Dauncey, 2016).

I have taken Wrexham as an example because it borders two English counties:

AuthSchool				2011-12	2012-13	2013-14	2014-15	2015-16	2016-17	2017-18	2018-19	2019-20
⊟ Wales				3,910	4,080	4,169	(r) 4,150	4,128	4,190	4,234	4,291	4,441
	⊞ Isle of Anglesey			3,652	4,184	4,513	4,349	4,264	4,302	4,457	4,409	4,557
	⊞ Gwynedd			4,097	4,354	4,496	4,490	4,517	4,499	4,513	4,538	4,653
	⊞ Conwy			4,217	4,387	4,484	4,579	4,544	4,602	4,567	4,598	4,591
	⊞ Denbighshire			4,218	4,513	4,682	4,675	4,606	4,655	4,799	4,832	4,927
	⊞ Flintshire			3,682	3,898	4,027	3,859	3,897	3,985	4,023	4,101	4,160
	⊞ Wrexham			3,859	4,013	4,102	4,107	4,095	4,158	4,225	4,306	4,425

(Welsh Government, 2017)

Looking at funding comparisons by authority on the first full year I did a budget in 2011/12 and with 2017/18, you can see the comparisons and the differences in terms of funding per pupil and while the Welsh Government will argue that direct comparison is not possible, it is clear to me that there is a definitive difference in the funding levels.

Year	Wrexham	Shropshire	Difference	Cheshire East	Difference
2011/12	£3,859	£4,695	£836	£4,612	£753
2017/18	£4,225	£4,466	£241	£4,340	£115

Funding is a pivotal part of how a school is able to manage its finances and operate effectively and while the funding gap between England and Wales has decreased it is still a cause for concern among school and unions (BBC News, 2018) (Wales Online, 2011).

With funding so tight in Wales, it was imperative to look at every single expenditure line within the school to ascertain where efficiencies could be made and to orchestrate these as quickly and effectively as possible to ensure that the running of the school was not put at risk.

There is no academy system in Wales and a smaller percentage of schools have a cheque book in comparison with England. Local authorities exercise far greater control over the finances of individual schools and service level agreements are very much the norm. I have always found it better to deal directly with suppliers to get the best value for the school. Using the consortium approach can reap benefits but you should always be wary of their potential not to deliver any significant benefit (BBC News, 2018), much more fruitful and collaborate have been the cluster approaches and buying strategies employed by schools.

Another difference to be aware of when comparing England and Wales from the perspective of a school business manager is the lack of structure in evidence to promote the benefit of the position in Welsh schools. Particularly acute is the lack of the school business manager role in primary education, many of these individuals are still seen as school administrators or even the school secretary and have not had the opportunity to benefit from programmes delivering qualifications such as the CSBM. In 2008 if I had wanted to access CPD training for CSBM, DSBM or ADSBM, from a Welsh school I would have either had to fund it myself or see if the school would be willing to pay, and at a cost of £3500 per course, this represented a sum of money too large for many schools to support. From my experience, it would appear that funding was not made available in Wales to support the embryonic school business managers suite of qualifications. Even when I had moved schools, the NCTL in England let me login as an international student which gave me access to a global network of school professionals.

Inspection of Welsh schools is undertaken by Estyn, who unlike Ofsted do schedule when they are inspecting, and having a little bit of notice is not as scary as receiving the call out of the blue. An Estyn inspector will take considerable time in looking at the school's finances and the strategy for improving them, which from my point of view is time well spent. However, having read many inspection reports, I think there still seems to be a general lack of acknowledgement that the school business manager is an integral part of the school leadership team.

This leads me on to status and worth of the school business manager. The Institute of School Business Leadership (ISBL) does sterling work in promoting the profession in England and now has over 2700 members and 157 fellows. In Wales there are only two fellows and 14 members (at the date of writing), an imbalance which I hope will be rectified in years to come.

Moving forward, the work of the ISBL in Wales will hopefully give some opportunities for those school business managers and leaders in Welsh schools who are looking to establish and grow their roles. Whether this is as successful and impactful as it has been for their colleagues across the border remains to be seen.

References

BBC News (2018) *Public sector bulk buy scheme loses cash.* [online] Available at: www. bbc.co.uk/news/uk-wales-politics-43293491 [Accessed 11 Apr. 2018].

BBC News (2018) *'Quiet crisis' over school funding.* [online] Available at: www.bbc.co.uk/ news/uk-wales-43345395 [Accessed 11 Apr. 2018].

Dauncey, M. (2016) *A quick guide to school funding.* National Assembly for Wales Research Service. Cardiff: National Assembly for Wales.

Wales Online (2011) *Schools funding gap with England grows to £604 a pupil.* [online] Available at: www.walesonline.co.uk/news/wales-news/schools-funding-gap-england-grows-1860893 [Accessed 11 Apr. 2018].

Welsh Government (2015) *FAQs on funding for schools in Wales.* (online) Available at gov.wales/topics/educationandskills/schoolshome/fundingschools/schoolfunding/faqfunding/?lang=en (Accessed 11 Apr. 2018).

Welsh Government (2017) *Delegated School Budgets per pupil, by authority.* (online) Available at statswales.gov.wales/Catalogue/Local-Government/Finance/Revenue/Delegated-School-Budgets/delegatedschoolbudgetsperpupil-by-authority (Accessed 11 Apr. 2018).

Business models and principles for strategic planning

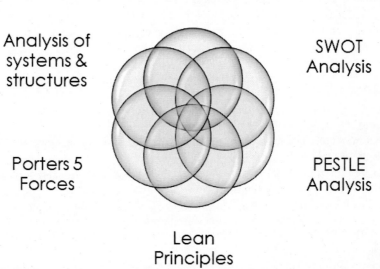

Due Diligence

Analysis of systems & structures

SWOT Analysis

Porters 5 Forces

PESTLE Analysis

Lean Principles

As a school business manager there are questions that we should constantly be asking:

- Where are we?
- Where are we going?
- How are we going to get there?
- How will we know when we have arrived?

These are difficult questions to answer, but we should try, and then use the information we gather to inform:

- the school business improvement plan
- action plans with SMART targets – Who? What? Where? When?
- key success factors
- project plans utilising Gantt charts to track progress

Due diligence

Due diligence is an investigation of a business or organisation, usually done prior to signing a contract. For example, when a multi-academy trust (MAT) is looking at a potential school to add to its group, they will carry out due diligence on the business elements and on the teaching and learning aspects. This enables The MAT board and the senior leaders to have a good understanding of how the organisation works, how it is currently run and its financial viability for the future.

When I first started as a business manager I was new to the profession and the school had not had a business manager before, but they believed in what was being said and written about what a difference having one could make. They were and still are a forward-thinking school and I am proud to have worked for them. I had recently started studying the Certificate in School Business Management (CSBM). I had lots of finance and accounting experience but I was far from being experienced in all the areas required of the role. For instance, I did not know what information I should be asking to see and review. It was a steep learning curve, but a great one. It is incredible to discover what you can learn in a short space of time.

When I took on the next role of being a finance director of a multi-academy trust, this time I knew what I was doing and what information I needed. I wrote myself a checklist of all the information that I wanted to collect and review, because as business leads we should have an awareness of this information, even if we are not responsible for the day-to-day monitoring and actions. There is so much information available in schools that can help you in your role as school business manager, you just have to find it.

Growth due diligence

As a finance director I am focused on the use of due diligence as part of the research in to deciding which schools should join the multi-academy trust, with two organisations coming together, the culture and ethos fit has to be right. To succeed, growth strategies must be planned and organised, ensuring that there is adequate capacity to provide the support needed. Due diligence is the process of ensuring that an organisation is financially sound and can operate and grow effectively. In the education sector this is why the Nolan Principles are so important.

The leadership skill with due diligence is to be able to question and challenge what you are given. The ability to read between the lines of what the information is telling you and not just take things at face value; appearances are not always what they seem. Look at what assumptions have been made in planning and forecasting, for example with financial forecasts and pupil progress data, would you agree that they are realistic? Are there any surprises lurking?

Due diligence checklist

Finance

- ☐ Financial position – budget plans, management accounts, consolidated accounts, capital account and balances
- ☐ Funding agreement
- ☐ Systems, software and processes – payment methods incoming/outgoing
- ☐ Debtors and creditors
- ☐ Census data – pupil numbers, free school meal numbers, looked after children numbers, forces children, English as an additional language, special education needs and projected pupil numbers
- ☐ Asset register
- ☐ Contracts – long term, leasing, subscriptions, licences
- ☐ Last audit report

Finance – Income generation

- ☐ Income generation – including lettings, wrap around care, clubs, uniform
- ☐ Grant applications
- ☐ Business sponsorship
- ☐ Incentivising initiatives *ie* completion of free school meal entitlement forms
- ☐ Marketing and PR – positive brand management

Governance

- ☐ Structure
- ☐ Reporting systems
- ☐ Meeting minutes
- ☐ Control framework – scheme of delegation
- ☐ Growth strategy
- ☐ Key policies
- ☐ Statutory requirements

HR

- ☐ Key policies and single central record
- ☐ Structure – hours, scales, job descriptions, vacancies, temp contracts
- ☐ Software
- ☐ Staff absence management and data
- ☐ Maternity/paternity/adoption leave
- ☐ Skills audit – Institute of School Business Leaders (ISBL) – School Business Management Professional Standards
- ☐ CPD programme and training needs
- ☐ Any on-going disputes, safeguarding concerns

Procurement

- ☐ Benchmarking data
- ☐ Software
- ☐ Contracts management
- ☐ Contracts and supplies *ie* catering, cleaning, MFDs, ICT, utilities, insurance

Land and buildings

- ☐ Asset management plan
- ☐ Site plans
- ☐ Condition surveys
- ☐ Building work planned
- ☐ Any significant problems
- ☐ Insurance claims
- ☐ Last health and safety audit report and inspection reports
- ☐ Asbestos reports

Further reading

Guidance papers are available from ASCL, the following documents maybe of interest to you if you are forming or joining a group of schools or a MAT:

- Taking the next step: considering joining or forming a group of schools (June 2019)

- Taking the next step: joining a multi-academy trust (June 2019)
- Taking the next step: forming a multi-academy trust (June 2019)

Top tip

If you are looking at joining an established MAT, their published accounts, which can be found on their website are a great source of information.

SWOT analysis

A SWOT analysis or matrix is a useful tool which provides a structured methodical way to evaluate the different components in any given scenario, such as a school, a department, multi-academy trust, location, product or service. The matrix is made up of four elements: strengths, opportunities, weaknesses and threats. Strengths and weaknesses are factors that come from inside the organisation. Opportunities and threats are generally of external origin.

Strengths and opportunities are helpful factors, which need to be maximised. Weakness and threats are harmful factors to the organisation which need to be addressed. Using this method you can identify the internal and external forces and produce a situation analysis which you and your colleagues can appraise to understand the context and factors, and from which a strategy can be developed.

	Helpful	Harmful
Internal	Strengths	Weaknesses
	✓ What are the positives?	✓ What are the negatives?
	✓ What gives us advantages over others?	✓ What puts us at a disadvantage?
External	Opportunities	Threats
	✓ What are the development elements?	✓ What are the external factors?
	✓ What can we exploit to our advantage?	✓ What are the things that would be harmful?

How can I use this in real life?

Start by considering your objective. Ask yourself what it is that you want to analyse and why. Perhaps start with a posing question, for example you might want to ask how the organisation can improve its communication.

Example: SWOT analysis of communication in an organisation

	Helpful	Harmful
Internal	**Strengths** • Website – compliant, clear, up to date, easy to navigate • Utilisation of social media • Staff communication – regular staff meetings and text messaging	**Weaknesses** • Dealing with volume of communications at peak times • IT – downtime, speed of connectivity
External	**Opportunities** • Introduce a communication strategy plan • Review digital analytics • Create a parental engagement officer role • Communication method rationalisation – reduce duplication • Introduce a blog • Purchase telephone headsets for reception staff • Design pre-approved templates • Hold regular open days • Provide a school communication guide/map • Research online event booking systems	**Threats** • Budget constraints • Policy changes *eg* information required to be published on the school or Trust website • Families – not having internet access • Complaints – reputation damage • Frequency that parents and carers change contact details

PESTLE analysis

PESTLE analysis is a framework tool for strategic business planning which can be applied to an organisation as a whole or to a specific project. It enables you to examine and consider your current position and the potential and direction of any change. By undertaking an external analysis and market research, you can understand the forces and factors which need to be taken in to consideration before initiating your strategic plan.

The model has six factors for consideration and analysis: political, environmental, social, technological, legal, and economic.

Put simply PESTLE is an analysis of the factors that can affect your school. Some are helpful, some are harmful, and if you simplify the language this model is a fairly simple concept.

PESTLE analysis scenario

Background information

You are the chief finance officer for a multi-academy trust (MAT). Your MAT has been asked to consider taking on a local primary school that has recently been given the lowest rating for achievement in the area on the Key Stage 2 results for the third year in a row. It has a falling pupil roll, a deficit budget forecast and a building that needs urgent investment. The headteacher has been on long term sickness for the last three months.

A new housing estate is being built nearby over the next three years, with the potential for 20 more pupils per year group, this would take the year groups to capacity over time. You have heard that the behaviour of pupils is poor and that the staff morale is low, although you do not have any evidence to substantiate this. The school is situated on a large plot of land and has many opportunities for expansion. Some parents and carers are choosing to send their children to another local school that offers a nursery provision and wrap around care, neither of which are currently offered by the school.

Requirement

You have been asked to produce a report that outlines your thoughts on whether the MAT should take on the school, including notes on additional information that you would want to review before making a final recommendation.

Approach

Below I have drawn up some notes, from the information above and information that would be publicly available. This would form the basis of the analysis and research for the report. In terms of asking for additional information to form a detailed response, I would want to see as many pieces of information and documentation as possible in accordance with due diligence procedures.

	Definition	**Example**
Political	What are the political factors that will affect our organisation? • Government policies • Government term, change, elections • Funding and grants • Lobbying and pressure groups • Bureaucracy	The falling roll is likely to be a factor in the deficit budget, a more detailed review of the finances would be needed. A large part of the area has high deprivation, but the FSM numbers appear low. Look at published information for finance ie published accounts, benchmarking data, school fund accounts on website, income generation stream information which maybe evident from the website. The current government policy is supportive of increased academisation.
Economic	What are the economic factors that will affect our organisation? • Local economy • Taxation • Inflation • Economic trends • Industry growth	Parents/carers are currently choosing an alternative provider because of the additional services on offer. Introducing a nursery and wrap around service needs to be considered and detailed costings modelled. Investigating prices being charged locally for similar services would provide a useful benchmark. More housing being built signifies an area of growth and investment. Investigations should be made to see if there is any capital money available for space planning. Detailed analysis of staffing and non-staffing costs. Maximisation of income opportunities based on pupil demographic *ie* pupil premium.

	Definition	Example
Social/Culture	What social aspects are there that will affect our organisation? • Demographic of population nationally and locally • Media views • School work ethic • Brand/organisation image • Lifestyle trends • Parent/carer attitudes and opinions • Ethical issues • Role models • Major events and influences • Advertising and publicity	From a review of the local media, the school suffered negative publicity due to poor results. I can find no positive news stories. Celebrating achievements and positive news would be a priority. A survey of parents and carers pupil voice and staff opinion would be a priority. As key stakeholders, establishing and managing their expectations would be important if we were to bring the school in to the MAT. To give the school a fresh start, rebranding would be an option to consider. We would need to take a more detailed look at the demographic of the school. Stakeholder engagement and consultation. How is the trust viewed? Will a takeover be welcomed or opposed?
Technological	What technological changes are there that will affect our organisation? • Emerging technologies • Ageing technology • Technology legislation • Research and innovation • Information and communication • Competitors technological developments and usage • Intellectual property rights	Having reviewed the school website, it is apparent that it is not compliant with current requirements, and a number of policies are out of date. A review of the IT infrastructure, technology, equipment, software, etc would be useful, *ie* site inspection and survey report, location plan, fitness for purpose, any limitations ie Wi-Fi coverage. The school has a social media page, but it has not been updated recently, it contains many complaints from parents and carers about the school.

	Definition	Example
Legal	What is the current and impending legislation that will affect our organisation? • Current/future legislation • Regulatory bodies and processes • Employment law • Consumer protection • H&S regulations • Money laundering regulations • Tax regulations	Investigate the nature of the headteacher's absence and what support has been put in place. Consider whether we have the capacity to share resources and staffing. A copy of the latest H&S audit report would be needed. Establish if there are any on-going legal issues, *ie* staff grievances, H&S breaches, legal disputes.
Environmental	What are the environmental factors that will affect our organisation? • Environmental and ecological regulations • Reduction of carbon footprint • Sustainability • Impact of adverse weather	A full building survey would be needed in order to review the full extent of the investment required. A full site inspection would be useful to identify the possible capacity for income generation to support reducing the deficit.

I am sure reading through this you can think of lots of other information, data and ideas to include, but you can see how this tool can be used to good effect to cover key business areas.

Lean principles

Toyota Production Systems first developed the idea of lean principles in an effort to improve cost effectiveness, quality and the timely delivery of services. Improvements are brought about by removing waste through *kaizen*, a Japanese word meaning 'change for better' or 'good change' (Jones and Womack, 2003). The implementation of lean principles should create greater value with fewer resources, a challenge being faced by many within the education sector. It is a systematic framework for minimising waste, for example by looking at unevenness in workloads or the waste that is created by overburden. If you analysed the workloads of those people in your organisation who perform similar roles, would they have similar workloads? How much duplication of effort would there be? I think that the possibilities of using this system in education are yet to be fully explored but it could be an effective tool in future research and development into improving economy, efficiency and effectiveness.

I have found in education that we often bring in new pieces of software or change processes with the aim of saving time, improving efficiency, reducing costs, improving the quality of information and achieving more timely reporting. Instead what often ends up happening is that we are entering the same information on several systems. When it comes to using software that works for us, we need to be aiming for a single point of entry or at least a framework where information can be quickly uploaded or transferred from one system to another. There is not yet a system that can handle every function that a school undertakes, but when one is perfected I am certain that its use will reduce waste enormously.

Think about your staffing resources and the cost of having a one-hour staff meeting. Calculate the hourly rate for each person and add it all together to get the cost of the meeting. Was the cost worth it? What was the impact or outcome of the meeting? Could the contents have been summarised in an email or briefing paper? Was it collecting feedback and if so could this have been done more time and cost efficiently by using an online survey tool? Did all those people need to be there?

It is my observation that in education there is a lot of un-noticed waste of time, money and resources. Where it is questioned the usual answer is 'Because we have always done it that way' or 'Because such and such a person likes it done that way' or even just that no-one wants to question it or has the time to question it. In response to my question 'What you would do if you had a free week to spend on anything you wanted that would make a difference to pupils?'

one individual said that they would look at everything they did, from catering to procurement, and identify where improvements and efficiencies could be made. I agree that reviewing and observing everything we do in a timely way, using the lean principles as a methodology could through incremental improvements transform the way that schools are run.

5S System – Jones and Womack (2003)

The '5S' system is useful in helping you to actualise lean principles. As shown in the table below, there are 5 stages to work through, and to keep working through as a continual process of organisational improvement. You start by identifying and defining process, from start to finish. In manufacturing terms, this would be say, building a car from start to finish, with all the component processes and supply chain arrangements.

The system can also be applied to much simpler systems, such as the procedure for processing an invoice, look at every stage from start to finish, how the invoice is received, how many people or stages the invoice goes through to get to the payment stage.

For example, you may identify that invoices are delayed in being payed because they are received by post by individual schools, before being sent by post to a head office for payment. It maybe more time efficient to have a separate email address for finance *ie* finance@ and ask for all invoices to be sent there and that the inbox will be accessed once a week by the finance clerk and to have an electronic process of approval.

Use the process to identify duplication, delay and waste. It is an important point that 'Waste' can mean the waste of money, time or resources. Think of yours and your colleagues time in terms of an hourly charging rate. Reflect on how your time is spent and the cost of each individual undertaking the tasks and activities that they do, on a day to day basis.

Stage	Explanation
1. Value	Identify and define – what is the value from the customer perspective? What is the end-to-end experience?

Stage	Explanation
2. Value stream	Map the value stream, undertake observations and identify all the steps, analysing which are adding value to the outcomes for young people and which are not.
	Identify and understand how work gets done, look at ways to improve the process yourself or with your team; or alternatively with another school.
	Looking at what we do and how we do it. A great example of cost and impact is available from, The Education Endowment Foundation (EEF) who have published interesting information which examines the correlation between cost and impact in teaching and learning strategies. Take a look at the resources available:
	educationendowmentfoundation.org.uk/evidence-summaries/teaching-learning-toolkit/
3. Flow	Create the flow sequence (the steps of the process/procedure) of the end to end process or service and try to achieve continuous flow.
	Smooth the peaks and troughs. Smooth the process. For example, do you have a sticking point in the process whereby things get stuck on someone's desk or in an email inbox, and it stops/slows the process?
	Is there wastage in the process? Are there more people involved than need to be?
	'Waste' can mean the waste of money, time or resources.
	Waste can come from waiting, over processing, defects, transport, inventory and motion.
	For example, if you look at your meeting schedule and content, do they add value? Consider the cost of each meeting, take the hourly rate of those attending, multiplied by the length and frequency of the meetings. This is your cost. Is it adding value?
	Think about these notions in terms of a school setting and in terms of adding value to the service being provided – that of educating young people.

Stage	Explanation
4. Pull	Establish pull through the stream – make the process run as smoothly and efficiently as possible. Make changes and improvements, then monitor the outcome – is the process/procedure quicker, smoother, producing less waste? Have you removed/reduced the sticking/slow-down points?
5. Perfection	Seek and pursue perfection, work on continual improvement and waste will be systematically removed. All activities should create value for the 'customer' through innovation and continual improvement. Aim to get it right first time, every time and you will cut waste.

There is much to explore with lean thinking and the innovation it can bring. Another example of a framework methodology which links to this is the 7QC which can be used to solve problems A Pareto diagram, cause and effect diagram, histogram, control charts, scatter diagrams, graphs and check sheets are used to monitor the overall operation and deliver continuous improvement.

Involving staff in the process of re-designing systems and processes, whether it is a business management or teaching and learning system can increase buy-in and ownership. Collaborative development, through continuous testing, development, feedback, optimisation and business planning will help you to develop efficient, effective systems which produce minimal waste.

References

Jones, D. T. and Womack, J. P. (2003) *Lean thinking: banish waste and create wealth in your corporation.* New York: Free Press.

Gantt charts

A Gantt chart is an ideal tool to use in work and project planning for scheduling and recording progress. It looks very much like a bar chart where each task, element and stage has a start and finish date. Tasks can overlap it they aren't independent with another task or action being completed first if it can be done simultaneously. It is important to get the initial sequencing of tasks right, as some will be dependent on others being completed first.

The time period is set across the top line in the first column, list the activities, how long each activity will take, and the expected start and finish date. Add in any float or slippage time available. List the activities in order of precedence and inter-activity, *ie* where one task is dependent on another task being completed first. Once a task is completed colour in the appropriate box. Templates such as the one below are freely available on Microsoft Excel.

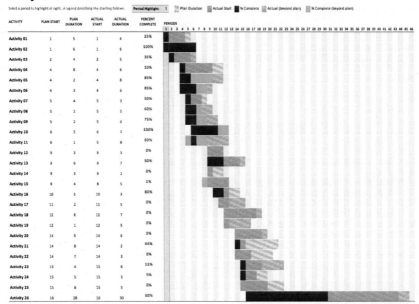

Porter's five forces

Porter's five forces framework is a business tool for analysing competition within your given business environment (Porter, 1979). Competition is an important issue to consider if you have a falling pupil roll or are considering setting up a new school. If parents and carers do not feel that their child is getting a good deal, *ie* that they are achieving their potential and are happy, they may well look to other schools. A good reputation is hard won and easily lost.

If you can understand the forces that can affect your 'profitability' you will be able to adjust your business plan or your business improvement strategy accordingly and market and celebrate what is different and good about your organisation.

The five forces are further broken down in to individual components:

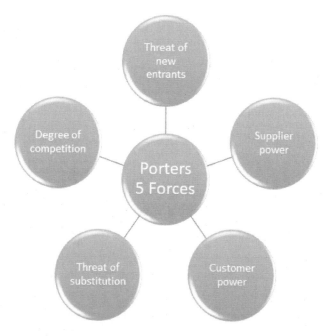

Force 1 – Threat of new entrants

- Time and cost of entry
- Specialist knowledge
- Economies of scale
- Cost advantages
- Barriers to entry

Force 2 – Supplier power

- Number of suppliers
- Size of suppliers
- Uniqueness of service
- Substitutions
- Cost of changing

Force 3 – Customer power

- Number of 'customers'
- Differences between competitors
- Price sensitivity

- Ability to substitute
- Cost of changing

Force 4 – Threat of substitution

- Cost of change
- Substitute performance

Force 5 – Degree of competition

- Alternative providers
- Demand/competition for places
- Number of competitors
- Growth opportunities
- Degree of achievement and progress

At first sight it might seem that many of these components are not applicable or relevant to school setting, but here are some points and questions that you could consider:

- How many other schools and multi-academy trusts are there in your area?
- What facilities do they have?
- How does the quality of teaching and learning and curriculum provision compare?
- What are their achievements and results?
- How do extended activities compare?
- How do they generate income?
- What marketing and PR do they do?
- What is the comparative cost of wrap around care?
- How much does the uniform cost?
- What trips and visits do they offer and what are the associated costs and expectations of whether all students attend?
- Are there any extra-curricular activities?
- Are there any provisions for specialisms in maths, sports, science, music, arts and languages?

By viewing your school as a business, other schools as competitors and the pupils, parents and carers as customers, it is easy to see how you can apply business methodology to your setting.

References

Porter, M.E. (1979) How competitive forces shape strategy, *Harvard Business Review.* March 1979.

Analysing systems and structures

> *The three C's in life: choices, chances and changes. You must make the choice to take a chance if you want anything to change.*
>
> Zig Ziglar (attrib.)

My way of analysing systems and structures to identify where improvements are needed and can be delivered, is simple and methodical. I use a four step process and when I am asked to take on a new project or to appraise a situation, I often run through these stages in my head.

Step 1 – Where are we now? What information and data do we have available that will inform us? Can we use that data and analyse it in a useful way using a business tool or model such as a SWOT or PESTLE analysis?

Step 2 – Where are we going? What is the mission and the vision? Do we have any specific objectives that we are aiming for and are they quantifiable? What is the anticipated impact? Will it have a positive impact on pupils? (If not, it is time to re-think).

Step 3 – At this stage I collate ideas and form them in to strategies and action plans, allocating teams, resources, time and money to deliver what was outlined in Step 2. The strategies and action plans will contain quantifiable measures (ideally SMART targets) that can be used to identify and track progress in Step 4. Providing accountability for improvement and demonstrating SBM impact.

Where are we now?	Where are we going?	How are we going to get there?	How will we know we have arrived?
Situation analysis	Mission	Strategies	Track progress
Information and data	Vision	Action Plans	Measure initiatives
Strengths and weaknesses	Values		Monitor financial results
Opportunities and threats	Objectives		

Step 4 – How will we know we have arrived? This is where the quantifiable question is important in Step 3. Can success be measured? Have we tracked the progress? Has the anticipated impact been achieved?

You can use this with your teams to forward plan work, look at cost saving opportunities, source grants that link to themes and improve budget planning and communication. For instance, it is important to develop a good working relationship with the person responsible for the whole school curriculum because its design is a major factor in the staffing budget. Any plans for change need to be carefully costed and considered. It is our role to highlight if the plan is not financially viable or sustainable. Ask your phase, department, subject leaders (depending on what term is used in your school), for their long term curriculum plans.

SMART targets

I was recently asked by a fellow school business manager, who is very keen to write a book, how this happened for me. This was not in a negative way, they were genuinely interested in the process and what they could learn from it.

I am very clear on what my goals and aspirations are and how I will get there. I spent time deciding on the one big thing that I wanted to focus on for personal development, and I spent time reflecting on the previous year:

- What were my successes?
- Where had I challenged myself?
- What had I done to support, challenge and champion others in the profession?
- What did I enjoy doing?

I really enjoy the process of writing, and of sharing ideas and practice to help others; and I have always loved reading and have always wanted to write a book, so after this period of reflection, I decided that writing a book was what I wanted to focus on this year. This was not a new idea for me, but previously it had been an idea, not a goal. I talked about it and made connections with people. I took small actions. I wrote an outline and a sample chapter. I shared the idea with other people and asked for their feedback. I ran a poll on social media to see if there was a market for a book on school business management and got a positive response. From talking about the idea, others started to show their interest and wanted to be part of the project. One of those people was able to link me with a publisher and the project moved forward.

Dreams and wishes are possible realise if you turn them into achievable goals with SMART targets. Whether they are goals and targets that you have set for yourself personally or in partnership with your line manager, you should try to make them something that you are interested in and that are achievable.

SMART targets are:

- Specific
- Measurable
- Achievable/attainable
- Realistic/relevant
- Time specific

If you are setting targets as part of performance management, aim to set two or three targets, below is an outline for deciding what targets to set:

- Target 1 – Link to you school business improvement plan
- Target 2 – Link to your school vision and values
- Target 3 – Personal development point for the individual

Top tip

Remember to link performance management targets to the ISBL School Business Management Professional Standards.

Business improvement plan

> *A goal without a plan is just a wish.*

> Antoine de Saint-Exupéry (attrib.)

A business improvement plan is your strategic overview of the business management function, demonstrating the challenges and opportunities that are impacting on service delivery and the actions that you plan to take. In the same way that the lead for teaching and learning has a school improvement plan for raising pupil achievement and progress, this plan will cover all of the business management areas.

Think about including the following elements:

Introduction and overview

Set the scene, summarise what business management looks like in your setting and the key roles. Highlight what your organisation does well and what needs to improve.

Vision and aims

Summarise what the future of business management will look like once the changes have been implemented and embedded.

Objectives

Create a bullet point list of the key elements, *ie* 'To have the plan agreed and implemented by …'

Keys to success

Outline what will ensure that your plan is delivered.

This could include 'Commitment of the business management staff to ensure that the actions are completed on time.' or 'That managers are dedicated to ensuring the provision of support and sufficient resources.'

Methodology

What has helped you to formulate this document? Can you refer to research and evidence that has been considered and analysed?

This could include:

- We have reviewed all of the previous external audit reports (finance audit) and inspection reports (Ofsted reports, H&S inspection, ROSPA inspection, *etc*).
- We have read government guidance.
- We have completed a mapping exercise and identified systems and processes that can be improved.
- We have completed a PESTLE analysis.
- We have surveyed and consulted with pupils, staff and parents and carers.
- We have reviewed complaints received in the last 12 months.

Identify stakeholders

Map how they will be impacted and how they will be kept informed.

Action plan

Set out the specific actions that you plan to take, with time scales, costings and resources required. Ensure the targets are SMART.

Action Plan

Remember that everything we do should have a positive impact on pupils, if not why are we doing it?

Action 1 - summarise the action in a max of two short sentences	Who? What? Where? When?	Resources required, ie time, staff, funding, equipment	Impact and success criteria	Evaluation - has it worked?

Top tip

Your own version of the document can be detailed. Remember to produce an abridged version for your governing board.

Project planning

View from an expert

Making something out of nothing, a tale of two libraries – Sarah Jones, creative and innovative project planning SBM, Send CoE Primary School

According to Sir Ken Robinson, schools should be encouraging creativity (Robinson, 2006). I think he was talking about teachers in his famous TED talk, but I don't see why they should have all the fun. School business managers can be creative too and I am not talking about in an accounting sense.

We all want our schools to be presented in the best possible light and to have unique advantages over other schools which attract pupils, after all, the bigger the headcount the bigger the budget. We also want the children in our schools to want to be there, to be excited about being there and to be happy. And that is where a good SBM can play a creative role in helping to shape the school environment into something a bit different.

Over the last three years I have been involved in two projects which saw the transformation of the school library from dull and uninspiring to exciting and magical despite the fact that I am not a designer or decorator.

The school has two libraries and for or each one the process was broken down in to five stages.

Project identification

Each room was initially far from being an inspiring library. One was bright yellow with turquoise furniture, the other had dirty cream walls and functional furniture. Both needed a facelift. The first step was to take a critical look at the space and assess its features in the same way you would look at a room in your own house, for example the purpose of the room, the light, any problems or issues, and how the room will work. Having this in mind will help your design.

Find a theme

Both projects had a similar basic brief – they needed to be accessible to all, timeless and tie into literary themes. To develop each scheme, I followed the same process:

- Searched online for other themed school libraries
- Set up some Pinterest boards to collate ideas
- Presented the boards to stakeholders (ideally pupils) to see which one they preferred
- Searched for props and thought about how they could be used to make the theme come to life
- Met with other members of the leadership team to discuss ideas
- Confirmed the theme

In this case the themes we decided on were an enchanted forest and a medieval castle.

Set a budget and establish priorities

Once the theme was established, a budget was set, in these cases, both libraries were to be completed for under £3000. Expensive items were identified, such as, wallpaper, decorating costs, flooring and furniture. These were our priorities.

In the same way you need to identify things that need to change for the project to work, you also need to establish things that can stay, either with some tweaking or remaining the same. For example, in both projects, the actual library furniture in place was good but not exactly in keeping with the new themes, so we worked with what we had. For the forest library, we commissioned vinyl stickers to cover the turquoise end panels and for the castle, the headteacher and deputy realised that if they painted the bookcases (which were castle shaped) grey they would be much more in keeping with the theme.

Start to think outside the box, particularly with more expensive items. For example, in the forest we put fake grass over the existing old and worn carpet as a cheaper way of enhancing the space, but in the castle the carpet was still relatively new so we just bought rugs and bright cushions to soften the space. Think about the entrance – you want to feel that you are entering a different world. In the castle the caretaker built turrets with a portcullis while the forest had a secret garden gate.

For each project we had a 'sparkle item' to bring it to life. For the forest, the accessories of the toadstool table, waterfall and birdsong were crucial. In the castle, the enormous throne for storytelling is the focus while the shields, banners and swords add to the atmosphere.

Source resources

Phoning suppliers directly and explaining what you are doing is surprisingly effective. Many businesses want to help schools and innovative projects can catch their imagination. Offer to share your project online and allow them access to images for their own marketing.

The walls are the most visual part of any room and the easiest way to transform a room is by using wallpaper. Adding different wallpapers to your theme board will help you decide which will work best, order a sample to see what it will look like and assess quality. I found that it was a false economy to buy poor quality wallpaper which had a tendency to rip very easily when being put up.

The internet is your friend when trying to find themed resources. Using sites such as eBay or Gumtree is easy and party stores are a particular source of props that can then be adapted. Once you have shared your ideas with others, get them to help you looking for items, it can be surprisingly addictive team-building exercise and I worked particularly closely with the headteacher when finding resources for the castle.

Implement the plan

Harness your skills base. For both projects I was lucky in that I had a capable site manager who was happy to help turn ideas into reality. You may not be so lucky but get the plan out there and ask for help. For example, you may find there is a decorator on the parent body who would help with putting up the wallpaper. Establish if your site manager is adept with a jigsaw and a paintbrush. Are any members of staff gifted with a needle and thread? Can your headteacher fashion an Arthurian round table out of MDF? It really is a case of the more the merrier and the more who join in the bigger the vested interest and sense of pride when the project is finished.

Finally, have fun and enjoy it. You too could end up with a dragon in a castle selecting his reading material for the weekend!

Top tips

Have a 'sparkle item', that brings the project to life. Local businesses can be supportive if you tell them what the project is about and what you need. Harness the skills and expertise from your community of staff, volunteers, parents, carers and grandparents, aunties and uncles, to support the project.

References
Robinson, K. (2006) Do schools kill creativity? (Video). Available at www.ted.com/talks/ken_robinson_says_schools_kill_creativity (Accessed 12 Apr. 2018).

Vision boards

> *If you are working on something exciting that you really care about, you don't have to be pushed, the vision pulls you.*

> Steve Jobs

When I am working on a long term project or goal, I like to use a vision or project board as a visual aid. When I decided that I was definitely going to commit to writing this book, I created a vision board which hung on my home office wall to remind me what I should be focusing on. It had quotes, pictures, articles and advice to help me stay focused.

I also use a project planning board at work, it as a handy space to pin up articles, plans, sticky notes and any other relevant information. You can move things around, cluster relevant items together, and add to and refine to your vision as it develops over time. They can be even more effective if they are used as a collaborative space that whole team can contribute to. One of the quotes on my board is from the actress Michelle Williams:

> *I'm hooked on trying out things that I'm not sure I'm able to do.*

That is what this project of writing a book has felt like. I was not sure that I was able to do it. I discussed it with other school business leaders and ran a poll on Twitter, which encouraged me that there was a market and appetite from the profession for this type of book. I was not sure that other school business professionals would be willing to give their time to the project. When I asked for their time and support, I was blown away by the positive response. Fear is not going to stop me from trying. As I mentioned in the introduction, I believe that is important that we create environments where it is ok to try, and it is ok to fail.

If you are ever in the position that you feel you are isolated or alone in your role, I assure you that if reach out to the school business community, that the support is there. You just need to ask.

Another quote on my board is from John Gray:

> *Understanding your own unique balance of qualities will give you greater validation, permission, and clarity to express who you are and to support others.*

This was relevant for me because I believe the best leaders have an in-depth understanding of themselves and they are reflective. It is these skills that help them to build strong teams around them. They know what they are good and what they need someone else to do.

Professional standards

The Institute of School Business Leaders (ISBL) Professional Standards document can be used for the self-assessment of school business management in your organisation. It can be used for performance management and career planning, recruitment, organisational development, and training.

The function areas are:

- Leading support service
- Finance
- Marketing
- Human resources

- Procurement
- Infrastructure

Each of the function areas is broken down in to a matrix of specific functions mapped against four tier levels. The tier level reflects the level at which business management is performing in that function area.

The Tiers give detailed descriptions of the expected levels of practice, from entry level (tier 1) through to those leading on the strategic direction of the function, perhaps in the complex and large structures of several schools (tier 4).

There are expected behaviours, values and ethics. School business leaders should be:

- Resilient
- Decision makers
- Collaborative
- Challengers
- Change catalysts
- Skilled negotiators

I first moved in to a role as an SBM in January 2012. Prior to this I had worked for a number of years as a senior finance officer in a local authority, and before that I was in the private accountancy sector. I worked for a national surveying company followed by a small accountancy company. During my time working for these organisations I undertook client accounting, adhering to the RICS client accounting rules I prepared sole trader, partnership and limited company accounts, along with VAT returns and construction industry scheme work. To support my accountancy and finance work I completed the Association of Accounting Technicians (AAT) qualification, followed by the Level 7 Association of Chartered Certified Accountants (ACCA) qualification.

When I heard about the ISBL professional standards I spent time mapping out my current skill levels in each of the function areas, completing a self-assessment exercise in May 2016. It took me a couple of hours to complete, there are quite a few statements and I needed to work my way through them uninterrupted. The findings demonstrated, unsurprisingly given my background, that finance was a strong area for me, along with a large part of the Leading Support Services function.

If you decide to do the self-assessment yourself, the most important piece of advice that I can give you is to work your way through the statements and assess them based on the whole function area in your school or MAT, not purely as a self-assessment of yourself. You may want to use it to identify some areas that you need improve on personally, but as business leaders we are part of a team delivering support services, and the self-assessment should help us to identify areas where we can better utilise the skills and expertise we have to best effect.

I am a methodical person and I like to identify quick wins, so I started with the area in which I felt most competent, finance. Next to each line I put the number that I felt was most appropriate. I decided to colour code my numbers because I wanted to be able to easily pick out areas for improvement. I also added a notes column and annotations of evidence as well as details of where another member of the team or an external provider was providing expertise.

Completing the self-assessment would be a useful tool to use to inform your business improvement plan. It can assist you in performance management discussions, identifying gaps in skills and functions, and identifying areas for future professional development activities. It can also be a useful tool in succession planning, and coaching discussions if you are mentoring an aspiring or new SBM.

Key performance indicators (KPIs)

Using KPIs allows you to set measurable targets that can be compared over time. These statistics can be tracked to use as evidence within your business improvement plan.

I have used the example of setting out your KPIs against the ISBL professional standards headings to demonstrate areas in which performance could be measured against agreed targets.

- Leading support services
- Number of complaints
- Average number of days taken to deal with complaints
- Pupil numbers
- Number of telephone enquiries

Finance

- Average debtor payment
- Average creditor payment
- Staffing costs as a percentage of income
- Generated income

- Income per employee
- Income per pupil
- Daily running cost
- The average cost per hour of a teacher, SLT member, member of support staff
- The cost of delivering an average lesson

Procurement

- Savings made

Marketing

- Number of news stories published
- Social media analytics
- Number of events held and funds raised
- Website hits

HR

- Staff turnover
- Number of vacant posts
- Number of days lost to staff sickness – this can be sub-analysed by role and department
- Number of staff absent due to long term illness
- Number of wellbeing activities
- Cost of staff cover
- Average time taken to fill a vacancy
- Training hours per employee
- Tenure – average number of years service
- Percentage of staff who met their performance management goals
- Employee engagement and satisfaction rating

Safeguarding

It is part of our usual processes and procedures in schools to safeguard, whether it be safeguarding money, resources or people. Working in schools we all do the mandatory child protection training and read the latest *Keeping Children Safe in Education* guidance from the government. We know what our duties are as professionals and as human beings who want to keep children safe from harm as far as we possibly can.

I still felt it was important to cover it in some way in this book and I found the right way, with this piece from Jo Marchant. Read the piece and think about what you would do if you were in this situation.

View from an expert

Prevent – Jo Marchant, AInsAM(Dip), Cert Acc, MBA, FISBL

Imagine you are walking along the corridor at your special school behind a couple of sixth formers (let's call them Michael and Andrew) when Michael says 'My friend told me last night that he is going to take me to Syria.' to which Andrew asks, 'Where is Syria?' Michael replies, 'It is that place where there is all the fighting. He says he will use my gun design and print it on a 3D printer and we can try it out together.'

You know that Andrew has a diagnosis of autism and that at times he finds it difficult to distinguish between reality and fantasy. For example, he thinks that what happens on *Eastenders* and what happens to people he knows are both real. You remember that recently there was a drama series on TV about young people travelling to Syria to join ISIS.

You surmise that there are three possible ways to react to this:

- Dismiss it as a classic 'cannot distinguish between real life and what is on the telly' scenario
- Dismiss it as adolescent bravado
- Think, 'I might need to make a Channel referral here.'

The last response would be the smart option. But, does it really warrant a Channel referral? You argue with yourself. After all, it is just a couple of remarks that you have overheard, and you do not want to get the student into trouble. And it is that assumption that the student will 'get into trouble' that could be the start of a slippery slope to radicalisation for Michael because the Channel referral process is there to safeguard students – which is why you need their parent or carer's consent to refer someone – not to punish them. It is there to prevent the possibility of radicalisation.

So, you decide that you should report it as a safeguarding concern and you report it to your designated safeguarding lead (DSL). Unbeknown to you, this is the seventh concern raised by different members of staff over the past month regarding Michael's comments. Previously, his class teacher and several teaching assistants have separately reported how Michael has spoken to them about researching gun design online and how he is designing his own gun. Michael has also said how stupid the school is because it does not have a 3D printer, so he cannot print his gun designs. Your report is the one that tips the balance and leads to the DSL making a Channel referral for Michael.

A couple of weeks later, you decide to follow up with the DSL to find out what has happened about Michael. The DSL has visited Michael's father, a single parent, and discussed Michael's obsession with guns but the father was dismissive and said Michael had been drawing guns since an early age and liked to fantasise a lot. When asked, the father said Michael had a computer in his bedroom and spent hours on it.

The DSL gave the father some advice about e-safety and suggested moving Michael's computer to a shared room in their house so that he can monitor what Michael's looking at. The DSL knows that moving the computer will not be easy because Michael likes routine and continuity. Moving the computer will undoubtedly upset Michael but persuading him that the internet speed is better in the lounge than his bedroom may go some way to smoothing the change.

The Channel referral results in the police sending an intervener to work with Michael. This involves him visiting Michael at school once a fortnight to discuss his interests. The intervener is a former seviceman and very knowledgeable about firearms and their production. He is very impressed with Michael's knowledge. The intervener's skill in engaging with Michael is based on his knowledge of how autistic young people relate socially. He knows that Michael does not like eye contact, will not be able to make small talk, and finds it difficult to form relationships. The latter is one of the reasons that Michael could be so vulnerable; he is a loner with few friends at school and he is likely to gravitate towards someone who shows an interest in his main interest – guns. Add to that his previously unmonitored access to the internet and you can start to see how he could be targeted by someone with manipulative intentions.

After three visits, the intervener is satisfied that Michael is not under threat of radicalisation. The referral is closed with the caveat that the school can always contact him again should they feel the need. The intervener's success with Michael has been based around taking his interest seriously, whereas most people have just dismissed it. The fact that the intervener has more knowledge than Michael about guns has led to a positive dialogue between them and an element of trust from Michael. The intervener has had the opportunity to influence Michael positively as opposed to him being influenced by people who may want to manipulate him into carrying out acts of violence for which Michael will have no concept of the consequences.

What is the learning here?

Take time to learn and recognise autistic behaviours. For example, people with autism often have unusually intense and focused relationships with objects rather than people. Leaving a parent in the morning to go to school is no big deal but not being able to find a beloved object could result in an episode of severe anxiety for an autistic student.

Be aware of their obsessions. If we are focused on their disabilities rather than their abilities it is easy to overlook the fact that such students can become experts on their chosen obsession. So be aware of their obsessions, take them seriously, and always report incidents that concern you.

Remember that making a Channel referral will be a process of collecting evidence from several different sources to build up a picture of what is going on with a student. Yours will be one such source. A Channel referral is in the student's best interests as well as everyone else's is because it is about being able to put measures of protection in place.

Finally, never underestimate the abilities of students with a diagnosis of autism or their vulnerability.

Introduce a customer service charter

A customer is the most important visitor on our premises. He is not dependent on us, we are dependent on him. He is not an interruption to our work, he is the purpose of it. We are not doing him a favour by serving him. He is not an outsider, make his problem your problem.

L. L. Bean (attrib.)

Many commercial businesses have a customer service charter that communicates the minimum standard of service or supply that customers should expect. School staff are involved in customer service every day, from the receptionist taking calls from various stakeholders to the senior leaders out on duty at the end of the school day. A customer service charter is a written policy that communicates to your stakeholders what you are committed to delivering.

It should be introduced as a collaborative piece of work. It cannot be successfully introduced by one person writing and enforcing it. The buy-in from staff is essential to its success, to help define the purpose, scope and standards of the charter and ensure it is written in simple understandable language.

Expectations should be clear to employees and 'customers'. Be clear on how complaints can be made and how they will be handled. Think about and discuss statements that could be included, for example 'We will aim to answer all telephone calls within three rings'. Is this achievable? Would this be between set hours?

Consider and test the ideas. Keep it simple, short and to the point. No one is going to read a 20-page document. Try to keep it to one page that can be transferred to a poster design.

Evaluate and report on results. Track data, for example the number of complaints received each week or month and the areas they relate to, and the average number of days taken to resolve complaints.

Human Resources

Not all readers are leaders, but all leaders are readers.

Harry S. Truman

One thing that many leaders in education and business have in common is the investment that they make in themselves, including reading widely for personal development. There is an almost limitless wealth of information available for you to learn from; you can spend time studying books about leadership, browsing the latest news and views on social media, catching up with educational policy developments online or drilling down in to the detail in research papers. I am not great fan of the word 'impossible', so I would instead suggest that if you have a particular topic in mind, you will find it very, very, very difficult indeed to not find any reading material on the subject. The following chapter was informed greatly by what I have read and learned about human resources not just in schools but throughout the business world.

It is people that make an organisation and their input and views are essential to its success. Obtaining regular feedback from staff, pupils and families is an invaluable source of information. Regular staff wellbeing questionnaires, surveying pupil voice, 'management by walking about', and senior leaders being available in the playground before and after school are all great ways of collecting feedback and gauging the mood of a school.

It is fundamentally important to recruit, retain and develop the right people to deliver the right vision. In her 2016 book *High Challenge, Low Threat* Mary Myatt recognises that people are 'Human beings first, professionals second'. She observes that good leaders combine warmth and understanding with accountability, and that authority and respect is earned through honesty and integrity. The way to innovate and improve, is by listening to and building on ideas from each other, not shutting people down or ignoring them.

One area where the business world has an advantage is in the ability to give incentives and reward exceptional performance. It can seem that businesses set their own targets and their own levels of reward, as well as having generous mechanisms for those who exceed their expected performance. But the issue of pay among school business managers and the education sector as whole is always contentious, as is any disparity which might exist between the compensation and benefits of school business managers and other senior colleagues. The opportunity to retain staff by offering flexible working options can no longer be ignored in schools. Jayne-Anne Gadhia, the CEO of Virgin Money reflects that as a new mother during her daughter's first year she was awarded her best ever bonus. She was working fewer hours and things were less intense (Gadhia, 2017). You do not have to work every waking hour to be effective and to demonstrate to yourself and others that you are doing a good job.

Inspired by the 2003 work of Tom Peters in *Re-Imagine! Business Excellence in a Disruptive Age,* Drew Povey encourages us to 'Re-imagine, don't rebuild' (Povey, 2017). He also references another famous business writer, Jim Collins, who states that assembling the right team should be our greatest priority in building any organisation. I would agree that schools should follow the same fundamental approach, that of people first. Povey's '3P' model describes the idea neatly; put people first, get them to generate the processes for how things will work and then the performance will follow. As leaders, it is our responsibility to make this happen, by giving people time and space to reflect and by providing the tools necessary to facilitate the processes.

References

Gadhia, J. (2017) *The Virgin Banker.* London: Virgin Books

Myatt, M. (2016) *High Challenge, Low Threat: How the Best Leaders Find the Balance.* Suffolk: John Catt.

Povey, D. (2017) *Educating Drew: The real story of Harrop Fold School.* Suffolk: John Catt.

Recruitment and retention

The aim of successful recruitment is to get the right people in the right roles. As Jim Collins advises, we need to get the right people on the bus and sat in the right seats (Collins, 2001). However, no matter how thorough our recruitment processes are, there are times when the fit between the school and the person, or the person and role, simply does not work. Our staff are our biggest assets, but if not managed and led in the right way, they are potentially our greatest risk.

Recruitment is a time consuming and costly exercise, but I believe that some turnover of staff is useful, bringing the opportunity for internal candidates to apply for promotions or secondments, and the fresh outlooks and different expertise of external candidates. Recruitment can be an opportunity to re-design, re-imagine, re-structure and even make cost savings.

Many organisations use values-led recruitment to ensure that the fit between the individual and the organisation is right. At a time when schools are struggling to recruit to key roles, we need to be innovative and use smarter ways of approaching recruitment and retention. This includes managing the school's brand and reputation so it is seen as an organisation that potential candidates want to work for.

Put together a comprehensive recruitment pack including the job description, person specification, recruitment process timetable, and information about the school and the role.

Organise recruitment activities well and remember that first impressions count. Plan a robust recruitment process that allows you to see the candidate in a range of settings and activities; it needs to be more than just an observation and a 30-minute interview. If you get the recruitment right it will save time and money in the long term. Utilise social media, teachers tend to look for opportunities at the end of the week and the end of term. Think about whether you are using social media and scheduling tools effectively, you can also use analytics to see when you get most views. Use your own personal and professional networks, just because you have advertised a position it does not automatically follow that the right person is aware of it. Can you give opportunities to those wanting a career in education by offering apprenticeships? Talk to colleagues in other schools, talk to friends, depending on the role perhaps somebody knows somebody who wants to move in to education.

Review the way that your organisation works and consider the following suggestions:

- Make your website candidate friendly
- Recruitment open days or evenings to showcase your school/MAT

- Exhibit at careers events
- Discuss training and CPD routes available for all levels
- Review your existing talent pool
- Link with agencies that provide general and specialist services
- Training centres
- Collaboration with teaching schools
- School-centred initial teaching training (SCITT)
- Support networks
- Shared resources
- Integrated NQT support
- Flexible options, part-time, extended programmes – don't exclude those who need a more flexible option
- Additional support for specialisms
- Resources for support and training
- Overseas recruitment
- Proactive marketing – for example encourage a return to teaching
- Advertisements – where and when to reach your target audience
- Social media – use a scheduling tool to reach your target audience at the right time
- Share information online about training, opportunities, candidate successes and pupil/school achievements
- Explore possible links with corporate organisations

References

Collins, J. (2001). *Good to great.* New York: Harper Business.

View from an expert

Peter Neale MSc FISBL, school business leader

Context

It is easier to recruit good quality staff at some schools than others. Over the years I have worked as an SBM in secondary schools in markedly different circumstances. One, an outstanding school in a desirable leafy area, was inundated with applications for almost every vacancy whereas another, with 'requires improvement' status in an urban setting, would often receive no applications at all.

Some schools have a settled workforce, with the majority of staff staying for years, and others have a high turnover. There are advantages and disadvantages to both situations: staff at a school with low turnover can become set in their ways, resistant to change ('we've always done it this way') and potentially complacent whereas staff at a school with a high turnover may feel tremendous pressure but have arrived with experience from elsewhere and ideas to help bring about positive change.

Many people believe that pupil progress depends more on the quality of teaching than on anything else, and that the most important thing a school can do is to provide its students with good teachers. The problem is that there are too few good teachers to go around. Many schools have faced recruitment issues for years and, coupled with difficulties in retaining experienced staff, have seen pupil attainment fall as a result.

In early 2018 the Commons Public Accounts Committee noted that there was a "growing sense of crisis" in schools, with teachers leaving due to heavy workloads at the same time that pupil numbers were rising, inevitably resulting in increased supply agency costs.

Attracting the right candidates

It can be difficult to gauge the level at which to pitch recruitment efforts, and careful thought should be given to each vacancy in order to maximise the number and quality of applicants for the amount of money spent. Finding the talent itself isn't as easy as it used to be: nowadays teachers don't just read the Times Educational Supplement to find their next role. You need to find a way to attract and engage the best people.

Being a great employer may no longer be enough: you need to let people know how great you are. You want your employees bragging that your school is a great place to work. People will believe the employees before they believe your corporate literature.

Having said this, your website is a crucial way of projecting your school's vision, mission and achievements, and your social media can be an infectious way of spreading good news. The employment section of your website should not only describe available positions but also contain compelling information about why a potential candidate might want to apply.

Running your recruitment efforts like a well-oiled marketing campaign – and using a variety of media, including local free papers for support staff ads – will help bring in the top-quality candidates your school needs.

Shortlisting

Selection for appointment should be fair, open and impartial. There should be no bias in the appointment of candidates and decisions should be based on merit.

In the past I have seen a plethora of daughters, nephews and cousins of existing members of staff appointed in schools (sometimes without even having been interviewed) and, while those individuals may be perfectly competent, it is always difficult to prove that they were the best available person for the job.

Potential candidates must be given reasonable access to information about the job and its requirements, and about the selection process itself. You must also take care not to discriminate against somebody under the nine characteristics protected under the Equality Act 2010:

- Age
- Disability
- Gender reassignment
- Race
- Religion or belief
- Sex
- Sexual orientation

- Marriage and civil partnership
- Pregnancy and maternity

If in doubt, always consult with your Human Resources advisor.

Safer recruitment

It is essential that you check references carefully and undertake background checks in accordance with the Safeguarding Vulnerable Groups Act 2006, and at least one member of the interview panel must have successfully undertaken Safer Recruitment training.

The interview

Your school will have protocols about who should make up an interview panel – depending on the level of the appointment often a Governor or Trustee will be involved as well as senior staff. Some headteachers like to take a central role in every appointment, whereas others will be happy to delegate responsibility to you. I find it useful to include employees in the hiring process; especially those who will be working directly with the new recruit.

Suitable lists of questions can be found online at useful sites such as The Key or The School Bus. I suggest that you set the questions at a level that test the candidate but don't try to catch them out: when I interview somebody I want to see them at their very best rather than uncomfortable and embarrassed because I have tried to trip them up.

A candidate is on interview from the moment they arrive at school until the moment they leave, and it is perfectly fine for you to ask the opinion of anyone that they have come into contact with – including students who may have shown them around.

The school will want to see how a prospective teacher works in the classroom, and it is also legitimate for you to set appropriate tasks for non-teachers. In an attempt to maintain high standards for all, one of my previous schools would set GSCE foundation maths and English question papers for all prospective support staff.

Selection

I used to say that if I had a choice between a candidate with a great attitude but without all the requisite skills and one with all the skills but a poor attitude, I'd take on the one with the great attitude. Bitter experience has shown me that neither may be suitable, and nowadays I'd have the courage to turn them both down. It's far better to make no appointment (and to try again) than to make a bad appointment.

Follow up

As soon as the successful applicant accepts the job offer, start to organise a programme to settle them into the role, so they quickly become effective – and genuinely want to stay.

Strategic workforce planning

Strategic workforce planning is a continual process whereby the design of staffing resources is aligned to meet the priorities of the organisation and to fulfil legislative, regulatory and service delivery requirements. The structure, experience and skills of the workforce should match the requirements of the organisation in order for objectives to be met.

A full operational plan would cover 12 months and run in line with the business cycle, so September to August for most schools, and would take in to consideration variables such as pupil numbers (projected growth/decline), demographics, additional needs, subject offerings, planning, preparation and assessment (PPA) time, release time and timetabling. Then there is the monthly and half termly planning, taking in to account factors such as maternity and paternity leave, long term sickness, and resignations. There is also the short term daily and weekly planning and scheduling, which can be challenged by unforeseen circumstances such as short term sickness, accidents, or bereavement leave.

A longer-term strategic plan might involve a three-to-five-year forecast which includes prospective areas for investment and savings. It is important not to underestimate the opportunities that come with change; a planned retirement is an opportunity to revisit your structure and see if there is a better way to deliver services. Plans should be based on knowledge and facts gathered through recording and monitoring quantitative and qualitive information, including understanding behaviours such as recruitment, promotion, turnover patterns, overtime causes, absence and productivity. Understanding the current staff and role profiles is vital, as is looking at succession planning and internal development; growing your own middle and senior leaders of the future. You should constantly be scanning the horizon to identify future threats, needs and opportunities.

It is important to monitor and measure the impact of strategic planning on business outcomes. If you make a change to timetabling, what impact does it have on pupil outcomes? If you invest in staff wellbeing, what impact does it have? If you invest in a whole school coaching programme, what impact does it have? Does retention improve? Does attendance improve? Does staff turnover drop? Do applicant numbers increase? Is the quality of candidates better? Every action taken should have an impact, and the importance of monitoring, recording and evaluating those impacts cannot be overstated.

Supply and demand in the education sector has been a hot topic recently, with some schools struggling to recruit to key posts such as maths, English and science teachers. When I was writing this section I looked at a well-known employment advertisement portal and within the UK there were 589 English teaching roles and 408 maths teaching roles being recruited for, even allowing for the spread across age groups and school types, these are still big numbers.

Below are the four quadrants relating to successful workforce planning and development: sourcing, value alignment, value creative and continual investment.

Sourcing	Value alignment
Recruitment Workforce planning Succession planning	Induction process (also referred to as on-boarding) Performance management Strategic planning and goal alignment
Value creation	Continual investment
Rewards Recognition	Coaching Mentoring Career pathways and planning 360 assessments CPD Leadership development

The ASCL guidance paper *Effective business functionality within developing MATs* (2017) is highly recommended if you are part of the strategic workforce planning team in a MAT.

Creative staffing

Creative staffing is the concept of looking at alteratives to traditional strategic workforce planning. Looking at the resources that you have available, identifying how things can be done differently, ensuring quality of teaching and learning, whilst still being able to balance the budget. It represents being a forward thinking school, who are willing to look at innovative and creative options, that others would dismiss as being against the norm.

I believe that recruitment, retention, staff wellbeing, outstanding professional development provision, and school improvement are all interlinked. I remember Jim Knight highlighting at a conference that smart recruitment and nurturing talent are key factors in successful schools.

Staff are looking for a value-added package, not just a pay packet at the end of the month. Many people are looking for family-friendly, and even life-friendly schools. As senior leaders we must foster a supportive ethos and environment and not just subscribe to the latest fad, fashion or buzzword. Know what your school is about and be clear about it.

Blank page

Start with a blank piece of paper and map out what is required in terms of staffing. Always come back to the needs of the pupils – are they being met? Could things be done differently? Would that make things better?

Specialisms

Do you have in-house expertise that you could utilise differently or better? Perhaps by designing and delivering training or resource materials, using their skills to support other schools, or marketing their expertise for conference speaking.

Train to train

Consider investing in training staff through accredited routes so that they can deliver training and provide in-house support, particularly in areas such as behaviour management and H&S training.

Sharing resources

Explore whether you can share staff with other schools, for example sharing the expertise of a language assistant.

Expectations of experienced staff

Consider the teaching allocation and expectations of the upper pay range and senior leadership scale staff.

Succession planning

Grow and develop your own middle and senior leaders of the future. Consider what opportunities you can provide for staff to acquire new skills, for example leading on specialisms or subjects, work shadowing, coaching and mentoring.

Induction checklist

Write an induction checklist and provide a new starter pack to go with your staff handbook, it will help managers to make sure they cover everything that they need to and will ensure that the employee has all the information they need to make a successful start.

- ☐ Induction checklist
- ☐ Staff handbook
- ☐ Relevant H&S guidance *ie* personal safety and evacuation procedures – perhaps design a leaflet with key information
- ☐ Safeguarding policy, procedures and designated safeguarding leads, along with latest government guidance
- ☐ Term dates
- ☐ Login details
- ☐ Useful contacts (payroll is a very useful one)
- ☐ Year planner
- ☐ Map of the site
- ☐ List of policies and risk assessments
- ☐ Key policies that must be read
- ☐ Staffing structure diagram or list of staff (with names and roles)
- ☐ Details of staff with particular responsibilities and specialisms, include the administrative, site and pastoral teams
- ☐ List of the governing body representatives and their roles
- ☐ Performance management and CPD process
- ☐ School development or improvement plan

In addition, information that is specific to the role:

- ☐ Job description

- ☐ Person specification
- ☐ Contact list including telephone numbers and email addresses for internal and external personel
- ☐ Dates and times of regular meetings that they will be required to attend
- ☐ List of pupil names
- ☐ ICT login details for all relevant platforms
- ☐ Timetables, eg moderation, monitoring, data collection

Welcome pack

The aim of a welcome pack is to make your new employee feel valued and secure and to help in deepening and growing their understanding of your organisation.

It can include anything that you like and is a way to show that you believe in looking after your staff and their wellbeing. It doesn't have to be costly and can have a big impact on their first impression of the organisation they have decided to join. You could include items such as biscuits, stationery or a travel mug, just small items that give a positive message. It would be useful to provide information about health and wellbeing, details of employee benefits, an outline for what the inset days will include, a copy of the latest newsletter, and details about upcoming school and social events. A nice additional touch would be to include a personalised hand-written message from the headteacher or CEO. It can be the little things that make a big difference.

Wellbeing

Without a focus on wellbeing staff, pupils and school performance all suffer.

Viv Grant

The virtuous circle of happy staff making a happy school which makes happy pupils should ensure that everyone is more motivated and more productive with a corresponding reduction in absenteeism.

Leading a whole-school wellbeing strategy

I was once set a performance management target 'To maintain the improvement of staff attendance, introducing new ways of improving staff wellbeing and refining the processes for absence management.' It was a difficult target to meet, but I am proud of the work that I did to improve staff attendance and wellbeing.

My actions included:

- Changing the format of the return to work form and meetings
- Researching initiatives that promoted staff wellbeing and costing a proposal
- Reviewing and updating the stress risk assessment
- Designing and implementing a staff induction checklist
- Putting in place a system for absence management reporting and the tracking and monitoring of staff sickness

- Undertaking a whole school stress audit
- Collating and analysing feedback from the staff stress audit, sharing the outcomes with the senior leadership team and discussing specific issues raised
- Facilitating team meetings to expand on the feedback from the stress audit. With the key questions being what is working well and what do we need to improve?
- Summarised information in to a report, discussed and identified actions and distributed the information to the whole staff

The data from the staff questionnaire was added to the results from the ongoing monitoring of staff absence and wellbeing, which enabled me to identify areas of concern. The clear identification of the issues allowed me to work with other senior staff to address and resolve any problems.

One of the most useful exercises I have done with staff is to facilitate information gathering through workshop style discussions, asking them to identify what is going well and what could be improved in a given area. The information you can get from doing these sessions with every team and department is interesting and useful. When you collate the information you can identify common themes. I feel that these activities done well can boost morale, staff feel listened to and valued, because their challenges and ideas can bring about change and improvement.

Wellbeing whole school plan

I spent a lot of time researching wellbeing and came up with some elements to formulate a wellbeing plan. These included recommending a staff led wellbeing committee, investment in induction, training and development, small acts of kindness, recognition and rewards, planning, and auditing.

Here are some ideas for you to consider:

- Staff wellbeing committee:
  - o Governor involvement
  - o Employee led, not SLT led
  - o Meeting each half-term
  - o Gives a structured staff voice
  - o Provide an annual budget
  - o Wellbeing charter

- Induction, training and development:
  - o Coaching and mentoring programmes
  - o Career development plans
  - o Mental health, mindfulness and growth mind-set training – provide staff with information on coping strategies to reduce stress levels
  - o CPD menu
  - o Welcome pack for new starters
  - o Making training and development the focus of staff meetings and once a term make it the only agenda item
  - o Managers available for one-to-one meetings
- Small acts of kindness:
  - o Have a list on the staffroom wall of what drinks staff like, so others can make one for them
- Recognition and rewards:
  - o Staff star award
  - o Attendance reward
  - o Wellbeing charter
  - o Staff shout out board
  - o Staff breakfast club
  - o Celebrate staff achievements and successes
- Year planner of events:
  - o A wellbeing week/day
  - o End of term celebrations
  - o Fruity Friday or Cake Friday
- Stress audit:
  - o Identify causes – What takes up time? What causes problems?
  - o Generate ideas
  - o Introduce 'You said we did ...'

This is an example of what a wellbeing charter could look like. It includes simple principles that encourage a better work-life balance for everyone.

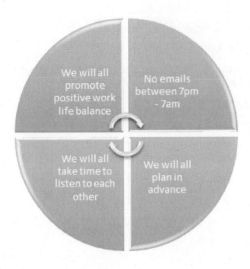

Here are some other ideas to consider:

Consider stopping all non-essential school email. We get so many emails and it takes time to sort non-essential items from those that require action; mailshots, for example often get deleted without being read. Instead produce a staff weekly bulletin, notifying staff of trips coming up, who is out, what meetings are happening, and specific reminders.

Only opening the school site between specific times such as *7am – 6pm* thus discouraging staff from working late in to the evening.

Producing an annual or termly calendar which is distributed in advance to enable staff to plan childcare and care for dependants. Delegate it to one person to control the school electronic diary.

Have all after school staff meetings on one designated night of the week and try to keep them to a minimum. Provide quiet places for staff to work undisturbed during the day and allow staff to have protected time.

Design checklists and templates for routine tasks. Share prioritisation techniques with all staff, for example if a task takes less than two minutes do it straight away, otherwise put it on a list. Start the morning by writing the top three things that you must do that day on a post-it note. Explore the use of other techniques such as the Diamond 9 and the Covey Quadrant for medium- to long-term planning. Not everything needs to be done straight away – have a long term list.

Identifying stress

According to an article published by the NAHT, the six core stress 'triggers' as identified by the Health and Safety Executive are:

- Demands – this can be from your workload, working pattern, as well as the working environment
- Control – how much say or autonomy you have in what you do
- Support – the encouragement and support provided by the organisation, for example, line management arrangements and governance
- Relationships – how the team dynamics work and how others around you behave, the culture of how conflicts are dealt with
- Role – whether the role that you and others do is fully understood
- Change – how small and large scale change is managed and communicated within the organisation

Reference

NAHT Leadership Focus Magazine (February 2017)

How can staff identify stress if they do not know what the signs are? I used to send a staff bulletin annually at the beginning of the academic year, that reminded staff how to identify stress and what to do about it. The Health and Safety Executive (HSE) describes stress as 'the adverse reaction people have to excessive pressure or other types of demand placed on them.'

Signs of stress in either individuals or groups of people can be exhibited as:

- Changes in the usual behaviour of a person, for example becoming angry or agitated, being tearful or with a loss of their usual sense of humour. Tiredness and being irritable with colleagues or pupils. Getting in to arguments or disputes.

- A reduced quality of work that is below the standard that the individual would usually produce.

- Demonstrating poor judgement or indecisiveness. Lateness and poor time keeping. Changes to their usual working pattern, staying later or taking work home, emailing early in the morning or late at night.

- Physical signs of illnesses, including headaches, nausea, panic attacks, aches and pains.

- In groups of people, there may be a pattern of behaviour or trend in statistics, including general absences, increases in complaints, high turnover of staff and poor quality of work or performance.

Your wellbeing

Looking after your own wellbeing first is essential. It is impossible to continuously help and support others if you are exhausted.

I am envious of people who seem able to easily switch off from work. I wonder if they truly do or if it is that they have wellbeing strategies that they use to help them. As I write this book I am the finance director of a three-school multi-academy trust, a wife and a mum. I took short maternity leaves with both of my children because I felt the responsibility to fulfil my roles as a family member and an employee to the best of my ability. But it is not always easy, when my children we were waking up several times a night, for feeds or because they were teething, it was absolutely exhausting. At the end of the day we are all only human.

I take my responsibilities seriously and being a reflective person I am self-critical of my role as a senior leader, I will often re-run conversations in my head that I felt did not go well to work out how they could have gone better.

We all have our own signs that our wellbeing is not quite what it should be. I seem to get a cold at the end of every half-term, probably because I keep pushing myself. If like me you work during the school holidays, these periods outside of term time allow you to take a breath and work with minimal interruptions.

Looking after all areas of our wellbeing is important and we should be aware of balancing our physical, spiritual, intellectual, social, emotional and occupational needs.

Self-care wheel

I attended a WomenEd conference on a Saturday recently. Yes, I realise the irony, I am writing about wellbeing and attending a professional development event on a Saturday, but their previous events had brilliant and were free to attend. This particular event was focused on careers.

One of the workshops was titled *Self-belief and self-care – the key to reaching your potential* and was presented by Stacey Adams, a chartered psychologist and lecturer in psychology who is also head of The Joseph Wright Centre. During her session she introduced us to the self-care wheel. The self-care wheel has six sections: psychological, emotional, spiritual, personal, professional and physical. Stacey explained the meaning of the sections and gave us examples of activities that we could try.

Here are examples from each of the sections activities and actions that you could try:

- Psychological – self-reflection, journal, aromatherapy, painting, read a self-help book
- Emotional – practice forgiveness, watch a funny movie, cry, find a hobby
- Spiritual – go into nature, meditate, find spiritual community, yoga, volunteer
- Personal – learn who you are, plan short and long term goals, make a vision board, cook, write a poem or a book
- Professional – take time for lunch, leave work at work, learn to say no, plan your next career move, get support of colleagues
- Physical – take a walk, safe housing, regular medical care, eat healthy, turn your phone off

We were given a blank template wheel encouraged to design our own wheel, that we could use at times when we needed to improve or focus on our wellbeing.

For example my husband bought me watch which tracks my steps. Using the benchmark that 10,000 steps is a healthy amount, I was amazed to find that on a day when I am working – a busy and tiring day – I was only managing about 3000 steps, whereas on a weekend, as part of an active family, I was easily hitting 15,000 steps each day. Using the tracker has made me more aware of my physical health and I now plan jobs to do which mean going for a short walk.

One of the challenges of being an introvert is the need for periods of quiet and calm which allows me time to mentally and physically recover. It can be hard to find that time. Planning time in my day or week to reflect, for example by keeping a journal and by using writing as a sort of therapy has worked wonders for me.

I am committed to finding a good work-life balance, but as with anything worthwhile, change takes time and effort.

View from an expert

Wellbeing for the SBL – @WorkingSBM2017

As he left for work yesterday morning my husband called out 'Look after everyone'.

'What? Really?' I replied. 'Everyone? 1000 students and 150 staff? No pressure there then!'

As a school business leader I do feel responsible for the health, safety and wellbeing of everyone in the school. I know you're going to tell me it's a responsibility that is shared with the rest of the senior leadership team. I know you are going to tell me that everyone also has a responsibility for themselves. I know you're going to point to the ready availability of tools, training and resources to build my competency to an acceptable level for my role. I know you're right, but that doesn't stop me carrying a burden of responsibility and it doesn't stop me wanting to risk assess everything to within an inch of its life!

In my experience as an SBL, having all the right training, policies, frameworks and procedures in place is only part of the story because we are mostly dealing with people, and people, especially children, can be completely unpredictable. I'll give you two examples.

Many years ago, a suspicious package appeared, tied to a lamp post outside our school sports hall. Nobody had seen it being left, the head of PE was very concerned as his hall was full of students taking their English GCSE and he wanted something done about it immediately. So, as health and safety lead, I swept into action and instigated our long established bomb policy, called the police and then got hold of the deputy headteacher. He came straight out, marched up to the package and opened it. KABOOM! (not) it was a box of local magazines left there to be collected by the deliverer. The deputy headteacher then went back to his meeting while I had to rather sheepishly tell the police officer who arrived a couple of minutes later that it was a false alarm.

On another occasion (at a different school) the fire alarm was activated just as students were going to lunch. They reluctantly dragged themselves to the assembly points within the required time, we ascertained the reason for the alarm, reset the system and notified staff that they could let the students back in. Unfortunately, they were all allowed back simultaneously, and I can only liken the stampede to the dining hall to a massive herd of wildebeest that have been frightened by a pack of Lions! Now, I wouldn't normally risk standing between a teenager and their lunch but we had no choice, we waded in to slow them down and managed to stop the charge before it hit the building.

These examples might seem surprising, but to an SBL they are very much part of the daily experience. The role requires flexibility, resilience, a strong sense of humour and a deep understanding of human nature, as well a firm acceptance of Murphy's law (whatever can go wrong, will go wrong). When you are dealing with children and (dare I say it?) teachers, you need to be totally ahead of the game and always on your toes.

So, with all this going on, how can an SBL possibly focus on their own wellbeing? Maybe I'm a slow learner but after fifteen years of being an SBL I have only recently got to grips with this one and set myself up with a set of tools to maintain my own wellbeing.

Look after you

Eat well, exercise, have a life outside work, take a lunch break, go to the toilet ... all the things we forget to do during the busy SBL day. Then at night, get enough sleep.

Build a team

A strong and resilient team is vital to the success and wellbeing of an SBL. They need to be flexible, positive and willing. They need to communicate well, with each other and the wider school. They need to be able to manage conflicting demands and to be built on a culture of compliance and mutual support. Keep succession planning in mind and help them develop their careers.

Seek out your own support structure

Every SBL needs a mentor. This can be an individual or a group but take time to maintain the connection during good times so that when the going gets tough they can be there for you. Keep your relationship with your own mentor on a foundation of mutual support and collaboration, but also make it known if you are available to act as a mentor for others. Be involved in local SBL groups and find ways of growing a wider network via the professional bodies, social media and professional publications.

Don't try to reinvent the wheel

Collaboration is vital in education today and it is important to remember to give as well as receive. Be professionally generous, you can always ask if they would cite the source. Make sure you credit anything you're using. Working together builds networks that will benefit everyone in the long term.

Even with my now well established wellbeing tools, I often think that the most important skill I bring to the SBL role is one of perpetual optimism. A positive outlook is necessary to maintain your own balance. Even though I know my team and I are making these things happen, I try to remember that; I will get the budget to balance, everyone will get paid at the end of the month, teachers will get the resources they need for the classroom, I will get the roof fixed before the winter, we won't run out of chocolate biscuits and yes, my lovely husband, I will keep everyone safe.

To read more from @WorkingSBM2017 follow her blog at: www. Workingsbm.com

Find the balance of your needs

Checklist – ways to improve mental health

- ☐ Provide mental health awareness training
- ☐ Listen and respond to the needs and concerns of staff
- ☐ Understand what the triggers are
- ☐ Be supportive – do not stigmatise mental health issues in anyway
- ☐ Model good behaviours
- ☐ Allow and encourage staff to work offsite where appropriate *ie* PPA, management release

☐ Facilitate a staff wellbeing committee, try to ensure that it is led by staff not senior leaders

☐ Implement a reward and recognition system

☐ Consider email restriction out of working hours

Make wellbeing, positive mental health and work-life balance a priority. Look after you. Build a team. Seek out your own support network. Do not try to re-invent the wheel, and remember, most challenges have been experienced by another school or SBM.

Flexible working

My husband and I work well as a team to balance the obligations that we have to our employers, our careers and our two children. We both hold senior positions and both do a fair share of the parenting, but of course there are times when it gets a bit tricky. For example when one of our children is ill and we both have important meetings to attend there must be an element of compromise. Schools with family friendly or even life friendly cultures and policies make it easier for employees to balance life and work and to fulfil their obligations.

Unfortunately, I have had more judgemental comments about being a working mum and the length of my maternity leave than I expected. It's interesting that my husband has not. Like other working parents and carers I am dedicated to my children, but I also get great satisfaction and fulfilment from working and developing my career. I have put in a lot of time, money, effort and dedication to achieve my qualifications and progress to a senior role. For those for whom university is or was not an option, there is always another way if you are willing to make sacrifices in other parts of your life.

I wonder how many great professionals have stopped working in the education sector because they found that it was not family friendly or conducive to a healthy work-life balance. This is a ridiculous situation to be in, when we are responsible for educating and setting examples for the next generations. What if we were better at supporting working parents and carers? Or staff with responsibility for an ill or elderly relative?

Often the flexibility is only needed for a short period of time. It is widely recognised that family friendly policies to boost morale and retain staff, along with improving productivity and commitment. They can also play a key part in attracting and retaining talented individuals and link to creating and maintaining a positive brand image. Are your senior leadership team approachable and empathetic if a member of staff has an issue?

If you would like to read more about this area, take a look at the bank of resources put together by The MTPT Project www.mtpt.org.uk/articles . Which includes personal blogs, news articles and academic research papers, covering the topics of: teacher retention, wellbeing, leadership, shared parental leave, family friendly working conditions, the pay gap, power maternity leave, returning to work, tips and advice for maternity leave and maternity discrimination.

How would you react if a member of your team asked if they could bring their baby to a meeting? This happened to me once. It was a day of the week that my husband would usually collect our children, allowing me to work later. On this occasion he was away for a work event so I needed to collect my youngest from childcare, which would not normally be a problem. Except that on this occasion we had a senior leadership team meeting which I knew was important for me to attend and I did not want to miss. I spoke to my headteacher and explained the situation and asked if I could bring my daughter to the meeting. After a quick discussion it was agreed that it was fine for me to bring her along. My daughter was happy with all the talking to entertain her and I was able to be back on time to collect my eldest daughter from her childcare. I knew that my headteacher was understanding. I was not someone who asked for time off every week, we generally had our childcare well organised and I was available when needed. This flexibility meant a lot to me, and it was part of why I worked there for five years.

Think about whether you need to improve the morale in your organisation. Reflect on your attitude to dealing with family related matters and review the policies and procedures that you have in place.

Consider the following points:

- Flexible working can come in various forms *ie* reduction in hours/days or a change to working patterns.
- Often staff who need to ask for a flexible arrangement only need it for a short or defined period.
- Consider what are reasonable adjustments to duties that are practical and enable staff to meet pupil or business needs.
- Job sharing.
- Secondment opportunities.
- Temporary or permanent change to part-time hours.
- Flexi time – there are roles that can be flexible, but it is important to consider the impact if you offer this to one member of staff and how it will be received by others.
- Working away from school *ie* working from home or a quiet location like a library, sometimes we need a quiet space where we will not be interrupted.
- Annualised hours.
- Maternity, paternity, adoption and parental leave.
- Utilising keeping in touch (KIT) days for absent staff with regard to important events, training and opportunities. It is important that the

member of staff feels valued and it can be hard return to work after a lengthy absence.

- Discretionary paid leave.
- Access to support services, including counselling, occupational health, mini health checks and flu immunisations.
- Emergency leave.
- Childcare, including crèche facilities.
- Encouraging healthy lifestyles, including cycle schemes, staff challenges and initiatives, wellbeing themed days – Fruity Friday, Wellbeing Wednesday and Monday Motivation – and classes (yoga or meditation).
- Family orientated events, for example, host an annual family picnic.
- Family orientated environment, including welcoming staff who have recently had a baby or adopted a child to come in for a visit.
- Training, including stress awareness, mentoring, coaching, effective CPD and performance management, induction programme, and the staff handbook.
- Wellbeing or work-life balance policy.

We all have a part to play in enabling positive healthy working environments where staff can make an effective impact on pupils' lives and fulfil their own potential.

Top tip

Flexible working can come in various forms *ie* a reduction in hours or days or a change in working pattern. Often staff who request flexible working only need it for a short period of time.

Staff absence

Staff absence can have a significant impact on our ability to deliver effective services, whether it be teaching and learning, caretaking, catering, pastoral or administrative support. Prolonged or significant numbers of staff absences can have a negative impact on the morale of the whole team. In a single small or medium sized school you are likely to know about any issues with individual members of staff. This may not be the case in larger multi-site organisations, in these settings the use of data and analysis is a key tool for highlighting problem areas. I would recommend that you record absence daily; enter each absence on to your HR system and produce a summary of the data at the end of each month. Note that I used the word absence not just sickness, it is important track all absences to get a true picture. Capturing and analysing this data will help you to identify the time lost to staff absence from work.

Managing staff absence

Guidance and advice on managing staff absence:

- Be proactive in managing staff absence from work.
- Keep in regular contact with absent staff. Make a note of when appointments are coming up and fitness for work expiry dates, it is a good reason to contact them for an update.
- Conduct a return to work meeting after every absence.
- Record all absences on your HR system, not just sickness absences.
- Offer a free counselling service to provide support for staff.
- Utilise an occupational health service, they can provide advice and guidance to help staff make a successful return to work.
- Use phased return to work plans to support staff returning from long term absences.
- Provide support and training, if someone has been absent for a long time there is a lot that they will have missed out on.
- Consider reasonable adjustments that support the member of staff and will meet the needs of pupils.

Absence management trackers

When I was managing staff absence I found it useful to keep a tracker for each member of staff with essential information such as a summary of where staff were in the absence management process and the headline figures of the number of days lost to sickness absences each month.

You can tailor this to the stages used in your absence management policy. In each column add the date that an action or meeting took place. You can see in summary how many members of staff are in the absence management process and what level they are at. I have also included an example of a typical staff absence record sheet.

	Level 1 Meeting	Level 1 Review Meeting	Level 2 Meeting	Occ. Health Assess-ment	Level 2 Review Meeting	Level 3 Meeting	Level 3 Review Meeting	Appeal
Person A								
Person B								
Person C								

Absence Management Summary Data as at: *date*	
Number of staff in the absence management process	
Number of staff at Level 1	
Number of staff at Level 2	
Number of staff at Level 3	

School Name
Staff Absence Record

Name:

Updated:

Sickness Absence Information:

Dates	Number of days	Occasions (rolling 12 months)	Reason	Absence Management Timeline

Total over last 12 months	**days**	**absences**		

Other Absence Information:

Dates	Reason

Absence Management Information:

Concerns: Improvements:

Previous/current actions: **Future actions:**

Any other relevant information:

Summary of monthly staff absence data

This report becomes more useful when you have data from a number of years. It allows you to monitor improvements or declines in the number of absences and identify peak absence times in your organisation, which helps with planning. (FTE signifies a full-time equivalent.)

Term	Month	Total number of employees	Total FTE	Total FTE days available	Total FTE days sick	Average days sick	Total number of employees long term sick	Total FTE days long term sick
Autumn Term	Sept							
	Oct							
	Nov							
Spring Term	Jan							
	Feb							
	Apr							
Summer Term	May							
	Jun							
	Jul							

From this data you can use graphs to analyse trends. Once you have data from several years you can look for patterns, for example whether there are some particular months that are worse than others. Compile a summary of this information to share with your senior leadership team and governing body. You can use sub-data analysis to dewlve further. Track short term absences and numbers of staff absent from each team. Benchmark against national figures, which are published annually.

Top tip

Staff absence information is a useful set of data to track, monitor and report on. Complete a return to work for every absence.

Communicating in difficult situations

Dealing with an individual who makes life difficult or who is angry, can be challenging and demoralising. You may not be able to change them, but you can choose how you deal with the situation and whether you let it affect you.

Control your emotions, be empathetic to how the person is feeling and keep your manner professional and non-judgemental. Confront the issue strategically and if you know in advance that the person is going to be difficult, have a plan. Clarify what they are expecting of you or the school. Try to understand how they feel about the situation and what the key messages are. If you need to de-escalate a situation, be aware of the level and tone of your voice, bring the level down and slow the pace slightly. Remember that you are giving off signals from your body, how you move your hands, the facial expressions you make, and how you are sitting or standing. Remember too that a little distance is useful, do not be afraid to take a small, slow, gentle step back.

Afterwards communicate regularly and send an update of your progress and any work achieved, thus ensuring that the person feels that they have been listened to and their views understood.

Discuss the situation with colleagues and ask for their advice. Is this the way that this individual treats everyone or are you being singled out? Keep an audit trail. Where arrangements have been made verbally, follow them up with an email or letter confirming the details.

How to ask questions without insinuating or attaching blame:

- How did it happen?
- Can you tell me about it?
- I am confused here; can you help me to understand?
- Can you tell me more about it?
- What can be done to help to resolve this situation?
- Can we figure out together a fair way of resolving the issue?

Remember that this situation will not last forever. Nothing ever does, people move on and new opportunities come along. Be patient.

View from an expert

Communicating in difficult situations – Peter Neale MSc FISBL, school business leader

You will sometimes face conversations with colleagues where it is necessary to manage emotions and information in a sensitive way. Handling these discussions successfully will help maintain a positive atmosphere at school while also enhancing your reputation as a manager.

Examples include:

- addressing poor performance.
- tackling unacceptable behaviour.
- resolving personality clashes.
- turning down an employee request.
- dealing with a sensitive personal issue.
- handling a grievance.
- informing a colleague that their job is at risk of redundancy.

The conversation usually takes place on a one-to-one basis, although it may be appropriate to allow your colleague to invite a union representative or a friend. For more formal conversations you may also wish to appoint a clerk to take notes. Your school will have policies to guide you. Although it is difficult to control how the other person will react to your approach, good preparation will improve the prospect of a positive outcome.

Avoiding the issue or delaying intervention

Instigating a difficult conversation can feel daunting, and there is a natural tendency to delay taking action in the hope that the issue will resolve itself without any intervention. However, if an issue is ignored it may escalate and become more difficult to resolve.

Failure to take timely action could:

- mislead the employee by giving the impression that there is no problem.
- deny them the chance to improve or put things right.
- affect morale among team members.

The best approach is to tackle problems at an early stage, thus preventing a situation from deteriorating and helping to ensure good working relationships are maintained.

Having a quiet word

You can help make conversations less difficult by having a quiet word with a colleague at the first sign that something is wrong. If colleagues see that you are approachable and ready to listen, they are more likely to come to you at an early stage. A small problem is much easier to resolve than a large one, and I find that an open-door policy works very well.

Preparation

When preparing to manage a difficult conversation, think carefully about some reasons behind it:

- What is your purpose for having the conversation?
- What behaviour by your colleague is causing a problem?
- What is the impact of that behaviour?
- What do you know about the individual?
- How will you manage the meeting?
- What do you hope to accomplish?

Write down what you want to say and be clear on the goal of the conversation. Check your school's policies and procedures and refer to your line manager or HR representative where appropriate.

Agree a time and venue for the conversation. Consider holding the meeting in a neutral place such as a meeting room where you can sit adjacent to one another without the desk as a barrier. Calling someone into your office may not be the best strategy because it will shift the balance of power too much in your favour.

Adopting the right approach

You may be worried that the meeting will turn into a confrontation or that it will not go as planned. You may also be concerned that you do not possess the necessary skills to solve the problem. Try to think of ways that the conversation will fix the situation without causing further issues between you and your colleague.

Handling a contentious issue will require a different approach to undertaking regular everyday conversations. Make it your aim to reach a mutual understanding through a mature, collaborative exchange of views and ideas rather than seeking to achieve a victory.

Managing your emotional state

Emotions can occupy too much of your thoughts before and after a conversation. They are, however, inevitable, so learning how to manage your own and your colleagues' emotions is crucial. A manager with high emotional intelligence will always attempt to limit any collateral damage to a relationship with an employee. Take responsibility for feeling the way you do, rather than blaming the other person. Be clear and specific about what your colleague did that contributed to your reaction. Rather than saying 'You make me so angry' focus on your colleague's actual behaviour.

Challenging your assumptions

Spend a little time reflecting on your attitude towards the situation and the person involved. Try stepping into your colleague's shoes and considering their point of view. Wanting the best for the other person is a good place to start. It isn't about winning the argument or using your authority to browbeat your colleague into compliance; it's about finding a win-win solution or, at the very least, an amicable agreement. Take care to distinguish between opinions and facts. Test your assumptions and be ready for them to be challenged

The meeting

Although it can be tempting to enter a meeting wanting to be liked and to maintain a close friendship with the employee, most conversations will work best if you adopt a professional manner. Set out from the beginning how the meeting will run, the issues you wish to discuss and how you hope to move forward.

Speak calmly to ensure your colleague will hear the content of your message rather than be preoccupied with your emotions. It would be counterproductive for them to feel threatened, so avoid insults, threats and finger-pointing; you don't want them to argue or worse, to storm out of the room.

Present your side of the story by explaining what has given rise to your concern and stating the facts clearly and concisely as you see them. Be as clear as possible, using specific examples.

You may choose to use a 'praise sandwich' where the 'bread' of the sandwich includes positive words of praise and the 'filling' in the middle addresses the heart of the matter. This method allows you to share good news alongside the difficult conversation and will help maintain working relationships.

Listening

Approach the conversation with curiosity rather than judgement. Invite your colleague to express their own perspective, listen carefully and demonstrate clearly that you are doing so. Adopt an open posture, using body language to convey that you are willing to consider their point of view.

Don't assume that you know what they are going to say before they've said it. If what they say differs from your assumptions, don't accuse them of being dishonest. Their viewpoint may well be at odds with yours for a genuine reason.

When your colleague is speaking, consciously listen to what he or she has to say rather than just waiting for them to finish so you can respond. Don't interrupt, except to acknowledge, and ensure you understand what the other person has said before you respond. If you're not sure what they meant, ask for clarification.

Even if the evidence is so clear that there is no reason to delay or negotiate, it is still important to let them tell their story. A good manager remains open and seeks a greater truth in any situation. Your colleague may tell you something that could significantly alter your perspective of the situation.

Handling reactions

Nobody likes to hear bad news, and during the meeting your colleague may experience a range of emotions. Whatever is said, try not to take things personally. No matter how well the conversation begins, you'll need to remain focused on the purpose of the meeting and in control of your emotional energy. By remaining calm, you'll help your colleague to stay calm too. It can be difficult to control your emotions if the colleague becomes confrontational or makes an accusation about you. Remember to remain objective and non-judgemental at all times.

If your colleague reacts strongly, be patient and allow them time to recover their composure. They may be embarrassed about their outburst once they have calmed down so reassure them that their feelings are understandable.

Keep to the topic at hand. Bringing up issues related to other topics or past events will interfere with healthy communication during the current conversation. Save those issues for another time.

Finding a way forward

Be prepared to negotiate, especially if your colleague has acknowledged the problem. Both sides may need to adjust their previously held assumptions and accept a degree of compromise. Once an agreement has been reached, clarify what has been decided, who is responsible for what, and set a workable timescale for agreed actions or changes.

Afterwards

Whatever the outcome of the conversation, it's important to offer support to your colleague. Keep open channels of communication and agree to meet again to check progress. Ensure you carry out your agreed actions in a timely manner.

Top tips

Tackling problems at an early stage is the best approach. A small problem ignored becomes a bigger problem. A neutral location for a discussion helps to keep the balance of perceived power. Remember to keep your body language open, we say so much before we speak. Distinguish between fact and opinion, keeping examples clear and specific.

Dealing with grief

Dealing with grief in schools is incredibly hard. Whether it is the loss of a child or an adult, it takes courage, strength and empathy to deliver the devastating news in a respectful way, honouring the memory of the person lost. I have lost three colleagues in the last six years and I can assure you that there is no guidebook for the right things to say or do when this happens. Keeping your own emotions in check as well as you can and trying to stay strong for those around you takes an immense amount of inner strength.

If you receive the news in the middle of the day do you wait to the end of the day to tell people, knowing staff have to go back in to the classroom and function? But what if someone else receives the news or sees it on social media and starts to tell people? All I can tell you is that each case must be handled according to the circumstances and as a leader you have to support your colleagues, pupils and families in the dealing with the news as best as you can.

Remember to respect the wishes of the family as far as you are able and communicate with them in an appropriate and sensitive manner. It would be useful to find out about the arrangements for any service and if it will be family only. Think about whether a book of condolence would be appropriate or providing an area for people to come to and leave messages and flowers and reflect.

In time it is likely that an appropriate way to honour the person's memory will be found, maybe with a plaque, a tree, a bench, a memorial service, or a fundraising event for a charity that was close to their heart. Always try to include friends and relatives in the decisions if it is appropriate, to make it as fitting for the person as possible. There will be anniversaries and moments that are meaningful to those that were close to the person, and taking a moment to recognise this and remember them goes a long way to showing that people matter.

Managing change

> When Leadership Council birds, the middle management penguins, and the chicks are all on the same page with regards to change, it is amazing what can happen, despite the adverse conditions.
>
> John Kotter

There is only one thing that I am certain about when it comes to working in the education sector, and that is that change is constant. Nor are things likely to stop changing. During my time in education, if you look purely at government policy changes, there have been countless new agendas and amendments that we had to implement or give our views on.

The National Funding Formula, Pupil Premium funding, free school meals for infants, capital grants, new curricula, assessment without levels, increased safeguarding measures – PREVENT and FGM, Health and Safety –

learning lessons from incidents like the Grenfell Tower disaster and ensuring that buildings are safe and compliant with the latest guidance, audit, the academisation agenda ... and so the list goes on, and I have barely scratched the surface with the items I have mentioned. It sometimes feels like we are on a constant Ferris wheel of change, where no-one gets off, we just keep adding more.

Quite apart from these external imperatives for change there is also internal change. When I have changed employers, there have always been things that I have wanted to change. Things that could be done differently or more efficiently to save time money or resources. But change can cause confusion, worry, anxiety, resistance, frustration, and even stress.

When looking to deliver change, it is good to start with outlining the need for change and recruit some early champions or adopters. For example, if it is change in IT, look for those staff with an interest in the latest technology, if they are persuaded that the change is good idea, you have your early testers and supporters of the project. Bring together expertise and skills; people who have authority and leadership and who are well respected and credible voices. I have experienced that if you do not have the backing and supporting of influential figures among the staff, delivering change is going to be incredibly hard.

I found that collecting and analysing data can be a useful source of evidence for change. For example, an increase in staff sickness absence or a spike in accidents or near misses are indicators of a need for change. The way you present that information can be compelling to the reader, for example presenting several months of comparative data in a chart form against benchmarked local or national data, that clearly shows a problem, can be powerful.

Be clear on the vision for change and the strategy that will be used to deliver it. It is better to be 'done with', than 'done to', so when it comes to change, bring people along with you. Appreciate that change takes time, it is not going to be happen overnight and accept that there are always going to be people who disagree with change and have a different opinion.

There are two books that I would recommend about change; 'Who Moved My Cheese?' by Dr Spencer Johnson and 'Our Iceberg is Melting' by John Kotter.

Stars in our school

At a time when recruitment and retention is in the spotlight, it is important to reward and recognise the hard work of our staff and to keep them happy and motivated.

Stars in our school was an event that I organised after a member of support staff suggested it in a previous workplace.

We invited families and pupils to vote for any individual or team from the support staff, who they felt deserved to be recognised as a star in our school. There were four special awards for the following categories:

- Shining star
- Staff team
- Rising star
- Unsung hero

The nominations were reviewed by a panel which included one of the school governors.

The catering team baked star shaped biscuits and we purchased some small awards.

After the event we put all the nominations in envelopes and handed them to the nominated staff, because it was really important that they see and read the wonderful things that were said about them and the difference they were making. There is something really special about being nominated by a young person or their family. The awards were small trophies that were a minimal cost and the announcement of the winners was made in a celebration assembly.

Professional Development

Continuous professional development (CPD)

There is a Grammar school in my area which was recently awarded 'Senior Leadership Team of the Year' at a prestigious national awards ceremony, for 'demonstrating excellence in strategy and direction'. One of the contributing factors to their success was the range of initiatives they were delivering to improve staff development. The list was impressive, it included a fund to support post graduate training, research grants for teachers, a review of staff engagement in all strategic planning, new CPD opportunities to help early career development, and media and external relations training.

I thought that the inclusion of the last item was particularly inspired. It is our teams that answer the phone and we are expected to answer all sorts of queries and questions, but how many of us have been given specific training in how to deal with the media when something bad happens? Negative stories or coverage in the press or on social media can grow and spread at an alarming pace, sometimes before we even aware of an issue. As you can see, a skills gap has been identified (possibly as the result of a specific incident) and CPD has been put in place to ensure that it is filled.

Professional development can come in many different forms:

- Traditional training and courses, either face-to-face or online
- Conferences
- Coaching
- Mentoring
- Professional reading – books, research papers, articles, blogs

- Local SBM group meetings
- Being part of a special interest group or panel at a local or national level
- Research and development
- Pilot projects
- Observations
- Professional development meetings
- Taking on a specialist role – the names and remits change overtime – an example would be the current school efficiency advisors (SEAs), fellows of the ISBL who are deployed to support schools in financial difficulty

Top tip

The best time to reflect and list action points after attending a CPD event is the same day while it is all still fresh in your mind.

CPD menu

A CPD menu is a plan of essential and developmental learning and knowledge building for each type of role in school. It is important that when a new member of staff joins the school/MAT team or changes role that they complete the essential training that is relevant to their role. The concept of the CPD menu takes this further to include, the elements that meet statutory requirements ie health and safety and safeguarding, along with the learning that is essential to your school organisation, for example, you may have designed an induction programme for new starters at your school or MAT. The CPD menu offers the opportunity to design bespoke modular training that are above and beyond the statutory requirements. Ensuring planned knowledge building, developmental opportunities and succession planning.

For example, the minimum training requirements for your site manager, may include the following courses.

Site Manager

☐ Child Protection (Level 1)

☐ PREVENT

☐ Manual handling

☐ Working at height

☐ Personal safety/lone working

☐   Asbestos awareness

☐   Fire safety

☐   Construction and contractors

The CPD menu shows in summary the whole school approach to CPD for all of the different roles in school. If you work in a large organisation then you could have a menu for each team; if you are a smaller organisation, you could have two, one for teaching and learning and one for support staff.

Here is an example of what a CPD menu for support staff could look like:

CPD Menu for Support Staff				
Site Manager	Administrator	School Business Manager	Teaching Assistant	Lunchtime Supervisor
Child Protection (Level 1) PREVENT Manual handling Working at height Personal safety/ lone working Asbestos awareness Fire safety Construction and contractors	Child Protection (Level 1) PREVENT Manual handling Fire Marshall First Aid	Child Protection (Level 1) PREVENT Fire Marshall Stress Awareness Procurement Safer Recruitment	Child Protection (Level 1) PREVENT Manual handling Fire Marshall First Aid	Child Protection (Level 1) PREVENT Manual handling First Aid

CPD monitoring

When I was responsible for CPD and training I found it useful to keep a file with a log of essential training and copies of the individual certificates of delegate attendance (with signatures from the delegates and trainer to confirm attendance). The log was the control sheet at the front of the file. It kept track of the dates of all the essential training, which allowed me to monitor and action the required renewal and refresher courses.

CPD impact

Good CPD has impact through developing knowledge and skills, making links, changing practice, providing feedback and giving recommendations for further learning that deepens understanding to mastery level. Initial monitoring CPD can be achieved through the use of evaluation forms, either online or hard copy.

Longer term evaluation will come from gathering and analysing data relating to the aims of the CPD. For instance, if some of the catering staff have undertaken CPD in customer care, how has this affected the number of complaints or instances of positive feedback relating to their operation?

Key questions:

- What was the anticipated impact?
- What changed as a result of the CPD?
- Was this information distributed and used by other staff?
- Was it value for money?

Staff CPD reward card

The next stage could be to reward your staff for completing their school led and funded CPD requirements, for example, you could set 6 CPD challenges for the year, including activities, such as: plan, undertake and reflect on a peer review, read a professional related book and post a review on the staff CPD board, complete the Twitter challenge. The reward card could simply be like a saver reward card that you get in a café, where if you have 6 cups of coffee and have your card stamped or a sticker on 6 occasions, you get the 7th free.

Staff CPD bulletin board

The staff room is an ideal location to have a collaborative information space for staff, it could include:

- a social media working wall.
- blogs and articles on topical subjects, bringing together different viewpoints; reading is the starting point, facilitating challenge and debate is where the real learning happens.
- professional development books with a wider scope than purely education, for example there are many books from the sporting world about courage, resilience and leadership.
- positive quotes and pictures.
- staff shout-out board where colleagues can say thank you to others who have gone above and beyond.

Coaching

The aim of leadership coaching is to increase your ability and confidence to perform your current role, develop your motivation and ability to progress, and provide an opportunity to explore barriers and areas of concern.

I have recently sought a coach, having heard from other female leaders of the benefits, with some describing it as life changing. It was important to me that the fit between me and the coach was right. I spent a lot of time looking at the profiles of potential coaches, looking at what and how they communicate, and trying to match personalities. I am a positive person, with an attitude of getting things done and not wasting time, if I am going to take an hour of time each fortnight, for six sessions, I wanted to ensure that the time was spent well with the right person to help me. If you feel that there are barriers holding you back or you have been unsuccessful in going for the next role, coaching might be the right option for you.

I signed up for coaching, because I wanted someone to ask me challenging questions, that I perhaps had not been asked before, and to explore my potential and possible directions for growth. If everything stays the same and if I keep doing the same things the same way, I will always face the same barriers. I was open to the challenges and opportunities that the experience could bring and it felt like the right time for me to do it. I am secure in my abilities and I have a professional confidence. I felt ready to accept the challenge and the advice in order to inform and shape my future. I have been fortunate in having amazing support in my career, and I want to see what I can do to pay that forward, especially by championing the role of school business leaders.

View from an expert

Coaching – Peter Neale MSc FISBL

As children, everything we do in life comes with a coach or a mentor. A parent or a teacher instructs and guides us along the way. As adults, this type of relationship is more difficult to establish. Coaching at work is a useful way of developing people's skills and abilities, and of boosting performance. It can also help deal with issues and challenges before they become major problems.

The most powerfully motivating condition people experience at work is making progress at something that is personally meaningful. If your job involves leading others, the implications are clear: the most important thing you can do each day is to help your team members experience progress at meaningful work.

One of the key ways that you can have a positive impact in your role is by operating more as a coach than as a manager; looking to develop others for the benefit of the school. Over the years I have really enjoyed coaching some of my colleagues and watching them develop and flourish as they gain confidence. Coaches tend to focus on employee development rather than just a specific task at hand. Coaching will build stronger bonds between you and your team members, support them in taking ownership over their own learning and help them develop the skills they need to perform at their peak. There will, I am sure, be colleagues at your place of work who would benefit from spending some regular time with you, which will, ultimately, give you confidence to delegate and reduce your own workload.

You don't necessarily need formal training to become a coach at work. As long as you stay within the scope of your skill set and try to maintain a structured approach, you can add value and help develop your colleagues' skills and abilities.

Coaching is used as a reactive corrective tool in some organisations, but in an increasing number of schools, coaching is considered to be a positive and proven approach for helping others explore their goals and ambitions.

So, what is the difference between mentoring and coaching? In broad terms, mentoring is a way of managing career transition whereas coaching is used whenever an individual feels the need to evaluate their professional capabilities, allowing for genuine continuous professional development.

Coaching consists of colleague discussions that provide the person being coached with objective feedback on their strengths and weaknesses in areas chosen by them. Discussions are led by the coach, who asks questions that allow the colleague to reflect on their own practice and set their own goals for improvement. Coaching can be a useful tool for encouraging an individual to take greater ownership of their career path.

Questioning and listening

Skilful questioning and active listening will allow you to analyse a situation and prepare further questions. A good coach doesn't tell their colleague what to do, instead they ask pertinent questions that allow a colleague to think carefully and come up with their own solutions. You will succeed as a coach by helping your colleague articulate their goals and challenges and find their own answers.

The best questions for a coach to ask are open, non-judgemental, and focused on useful outcomes:

- What are your three biggest priorities for the upcoming year?
- What did you accomplish this week?
- Tell me about your experience with ...
- How would you approach that differently next time?
- What's the first step you need to take to reach your goal?
- What's the worst that can happen, and can you handle that?

Active listening is key to effective coaching. A good coach will listen attentively to their colleague and observe their body language, gaining valuable insight into their frame of mind.

Don't automatically assume that your colleague's situation is identical to any other you have encountered. Give them your full attention and take in any information that will lead to insightful, personalised guidance.

It requires skill to build the trust and rapport that will truly allow your colleague to find their own solutions, feel comfortable with the chance to reflect on what went wrong and how they can put it right, and feel safe with sharing their innermost thoughts. Try hard to silence any impulses you have to provide them with all the answers.

Reflection and empathy

Ideally you will maintain an unconditional positive regard for your colleague, which may be easier said than done. Throughout the process you should be supportive and non-judgemental; telling someone how to improve will not encourage their self-reflection. You can provide options and make recommendations but, ultimately, any decision should be led by your colleague. Encourage them to focus on what they are good at and to find ways to use their strengths to enhance their learning.

Analysis and feedback

Build connections between your colleague's role and the school's objectives and help your colleague learn and grow on an ongoing basis by providing timely feedback on a regular basis. Follow-up is critical to build trust and to make your coaching more effective. The more support you provide for your colleague's developmental plans, the more productive your coaching becomes, the more engaged you become and the more your colleague's trust in you grows. Manage the relationship to ensure that your colleague receives an appropriate level of support over a reasonable period of time.

Try to ensure that your colleague does not develop too much dependency on the coaching relationship, and don't worry about them becoming so confident that they apply for work elsewhere; after all, as the saying goes, if you love somebody you should set them free!

Top tips

Coaching is a useful way to develop people's skills and abilities, boosting performance and confidence. It is a personal and meaningful journey led by skilful questioning and active listening.

GROW coaching model

This is a framework for enabling productive coaching conversations in any situation and has four simple stages.

Stage 1

Establishing the goal, agreeing what the topic of your discussion is going to be and coming up with a specific objective.

Stage 2

Accepting the reality of the situation right now, by undertaking a self-assessment, reflecting and feeding back.

Stage 3

Considering the options available. It is important that suggestions come from the coachee and that any suggestions from you are there for reflection, not to give an answer.

Stage 4

Ending with a commitment to actions and agreeing any requirement for future support.

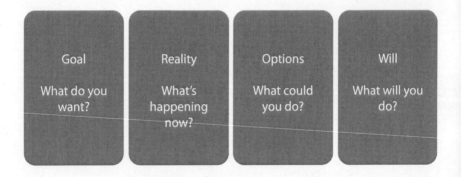

Your professional development

Professional development comes in many forms:

- Taught courses
- Conferences
- Workshops
- Self-directed learning
- Reading – books, magazines, journals
- Coaching
- Mentoring
- Online – social media, webinars, blogs, online modules
- Peer-to-peer support
- Research
- Networking
- Academic writing
- Emotional intelligence, profiling techniques and self-assessment
- Audit feedback
- Professional development reviews

A question I am frequently asked is 'What course should I do for my professional development?' It's a tricky question to answer because there are a number of factors to consider:

- What is your current role?
- What knowledge and expertise do you need to gain fulfi your role effectively?
- What are the skills and expertise gaps in your team?
- Where are the gaps in your knowledge?
- What role do you aspire to go for next? And after that?
- Do you want to do the training or are you being directed to by your employer?
- Are you going to be paying for training yourself? Will your employer pay in full or make a contribution? Is there external funding available?
- Are you expecting to do part or all of your studying in your own time? How much time do you have available? Are you willing and able to use your evenings and weekends?

- Will the course fill your knowledge gaps?
- What study method do you prefer? Face-to-face? Online? Classroom?
- Will the course meet the current needs of the school or is it for the role you want in the future?
- If you do the course, how is it beneficial to your day job?
- If you need to travel to the training, who will pay the travel costs and if required the accommodation costs?
- Are you planning to change your employer during the course? Will you be asked to sign a training contract and pay back costs?

Training can be costly and time consuming. It is important to take these factors in to consideration before you embark on specific professional development rather than find yourself half-way through a course that you do not have the time to complete.

View from an expert

Professional Development – Nickii Messer, school business management and leadership consultant; operational lead Anglia Ruskin University ILM SBM diploma programmes

As a school business management and leadership consultant, part of my role involves working as operational lead for Anglia Ruskin University's ILM (Institute of Leadership and Management) school business management diploma programmes. You would expect me, therefore, to extol the virtues of formal professional development for SBM and SBLs, and I do. But the reason behind what is a wholehearted endorsement, is that I regularly witness the immense improvement in professional practice and confidence that comes from such programmes. Even for seasoned SBLs there is always something to learn, and new skills, concepts and techniques to apply in order to improve the way we work. Certainly, for anyone new to the profession and trying to better understand this weird and wonderful world of education, such formal qualifications are absolutely invaluable.

There are a plethora of training programmes and qualifications to choose from, and most support personal as well as professional development. Choosing which is right for you can at times seem very confusing. While there are many benefits to having such a range of different options, you can also feel somewhat spoilt for choice.

My advice is, first and foremost, to determine that you will follow some kind of formal professional development route. To be a really effective school business leader, and to have the credibility of being part of the senior leadership team, it is essential that you do so. Once you have made that decision you will find the rest quickly falls into place. The next step is to conduct a self-review to establish your starting point, ideally using a framework such as the ISBL professional standards to do this objectively. From this you can construct a professional development plan for yourself, highlighting the areas that you most need or want to develop, based on your professional career requirements. It is also worth asking around for advice. Ask organisations such as ASCL and ISBL, as well as your local SBL networking group for recommendations and decide which qualifications most suit your needs and interest you. You are going to have to invest a lot of time into anything worthwhile, so it is much easier if it is something that you will enjoy doing.

Alongside any formal professional qualifications or training programmes that you follow, you must also keep yourself up to date with school business management and compliance issues, as well as the world of teaching and learning in general. Reading and researching should be a regular part of your working day, and don't forget to include the DfE website, education white papers and the latest Ofsted framework. It is important to remember that whatever we may think of as the business of the school, the real business of any school setting is teaching and learning, and the improving of children's life chances. So, make it your business to gain the skills, knowledge and understanding to contribute to this in the very best way that you can. The children in your school deserve nothing less.

Continuing professional development for school business managers – Jo Marchant, AInsAM(Dip), Cert Acc, MBA, FISBL, school business leader

I love learning and I'm grateful that I work in a learning environment every day. I particularly love learning that makes a difference to how well I'm able to do my job at school. Two years ago, I was promoted from school business manager to strategic business leader and I now work at the level of a deputy principal with input into teaching and learning decisions. Having been a manager, I decided I'd better learn about leadership so I enrolled on a master's degree course with Henley Business School. And that really tells you what my CPD strategy is. I look ahead to see what's coming next, I identify what training I think I'm going to need, and then I go out and get it.

Of course, a lot of training comes at a cost and I'm always very mindful of our training budget. With my master's degree, I applied for and was granted a part bursary for which I was very grateful. I funded the rest myself because I believe in investing in my future. Recently I did some consultancy work which my school was paid for and I wanted to do a 'Speaking with Impact' course so I asked my principal if the money I earned for the school could be used to pay for my course. The answer was 'yes' which resulted in positive outcomes for everyone because I was able to attend the course and then share my learning with the SLT.

However, CPD doesn't always need to be in the form of a formal training course. There are many opportunities available in school to which I invite myself. For instance, I've sat in on lesson observations to gain a better understanding of teaching and learning. I've attended inset training for TAs on the TEACCH autism programme to learn about classroom layout and lesson planning for autistic pupils and I've been to workshops about our new curriculum for pupils with profound and multiple learning difficulties. All of these opportunities enhance my knowledge of what's going on in the classroom and when I'm asked to fund resources relating to each of these areas, I understand how they will be used and am correspondingly motivated to find that money.

Skills analysis

Skill analysis is an evaluation tool for determining training needs, using a competency analysis framework or tool to identify skills gaps in the organisation. The framework defines the skills and knowledge required to complete a set of tasks and can be used with an individual, a group or a whole organisation. When things are going well it can be used for improvement and when things are going wrong it can be used to put them right. By assessing knowledge, skill, ability, attitude and behaviour the outcomes can inform training programmes, succession planning, recruitment, mentoring and coaching initiatives.

There are a number of readily available tools to help you run a skills analysis on yourself and your team members. As well as identifying any areas for improvement in performance this will assist in enabling you to understand yourself and your team, as individuals and as a group. Understanding other people better in order to harness their individual skills and knowledge to best effect is a vital part of effective team leadership.

ISBL school business management professional standards

The Institute of Schools Business Leadership (ISBL) produced the school business management professional standards with significant input from practitioners. The ISBL standards can be used as a whole or you can use a specific section individually. For example, you could take the human resources section and use it with your HR manager to look at the skills gaps of the individuals or the team as a whole, identifying areas to include in future performance management and training schedules. Information about the standards, including case studies is available on the ISBL website.

Leadership Matters

Leadership Matters have designed a 360-degree peer review tool called LM 360. This review gives you an insight in to your qualities as a leader via a self-review, where you will identify your areas of strength and those that require improvement, along with a peer review. I have completed this and asked trusted colleagues for honest feedback, which I found incredibly useful because it was not purely a performance assessment from my line manager. I included my peers and people working in my team, to survey a range of views.

MBTI

The Myers-Briggs Type Indicator (MBTI) is a self-questionnaire, there are 16 different 'types', which are described by four letters which represent four words, with one being taken from each of the following four pairs: extraversion/introversion; sensing/intuition; thinking/feeling and judging/perceiving. For example, my type is ISTJ which is introversion, sensing, thinking and judging. It is a well-used and recognised tool in the business world and help you in understanding how you make decisions and how you perceive the world around you.

Packtypes

Packtypes is an interesting tool that I was introduced to at my previous school and have also used with my current team. It is a simple psychometric card game that can be completed in minutes, especially when you have done it once and understand the concept. You can see who is focused on care and people or facts and figures, who the risk takers are and who sticks to the rules. It can help with understanding people and relationships, with particular reference to areas like communication, where it can assist in identifying the personality types who work better communicating face-to-face, and those who benefit from written communications. All the words in the game are positive and therefore it focuses on strengths.

View from an expert

Managing change – Peter Neale MSc FISBL, school business leader

Determining the need for change

Change in schools takes many different forms, from a new build to an academy conversion and from staff redundancy to the introduction of a new finance system. Sometimes change is imposed by outside factors, such as statute, the local authority, the regional commissioner, or a threat posed by the successful opening of a free school nearby. At other times, change comes from within, perhaps to reflect a new headteacher's vision, to react to a poor Ofsted inspection or to cater for significant changes in pupil numbers.

In most cases change will be initiated by the school leadership team and governors, and SBMs will have a pivotal role to play in informing their debate.

At the outset, school leaders will need to ask themselves:

- What do we want to achieve?

- Who is affected, and how will they react to it?
- How much of this change can we achieve ourselves, and what do we need help with?
- Do we strongly believe this change will enhance the school?
- What are similar schools doing?
- Are we prepared to be patient and diligent? Change could take a considerable amount of time.
- How will we know that the change has been achieved?

Change usually has unintended as well as planned consequences, and there is no point in bringing in change for change's sake. Ideally, change will be initiated as a result of a considered strategic auditing process. As a manager your best approach is to create a culture that embraces change, where change is seen as an ever-present and essential part of school life.

Developing the case for change

Once the decision has been made to go ahead, school leaders should draw up an implementation plan. This breaks down each element of the proposed change into identifiable steps, assigns each step to a person or team and suggests when each step will be completed. An example of an implementation plan is a Gantt chart, often used for building projects but useful in many different situations.

At this stage you can involve key members of staff as change agents. An effective change agent:

- believes change is possible.
- focuses on goals and outcomes.
- is motivated and resilient.
- communicates well.
- is flexible and creative, and prepared to think of different options.

Think about your colleagues, who displays these characteristics, and how can you get them involved?

Communicating the vision for change

Communicating effectively with staff, students, parents and, if necessary, the wider community is vital throughout the change process.

Change can be unsettling and in your role as an SBM you will need to be a calming influence. Be clear about what it is you are communicating and the message you want others to receive. Think it through in detail and then plan the words, timing, approach and style of the communication.

There is a balance to be struck between telling everybody everything straight away and planning change behind a veil of secrecy. People appreciate honesty and having their voice heard, and carefully handled conversations presenting a compelling narrative will give everyone a chance to understand the implications and feasibility of the plans. Consulting with people can also generate some very good ideas.

Don't assume that people have heard what you think you have said. Ask open questions to check they have the same understanding as you and make sure that you will have plenty of future opportunities to carry on the conversation. I find an open-door policy to be effective.

There will always be some who disagree with the change and genuinely dislike what you are doing. Try to understand what might be really worrying them. Does your plan have some real weaknesses? Could their concerns have some basis? Are they worried about their own capacity or skills? While they might not want to admit it, is it possible that they feel they don't have the ability or knowledge necessary?

Your first message should not be, 'Here's what's happening, and here's what you should think about it.' This approach will only create additional resistance. Instead, look at the change through the eyes of each department or person, and give them all time to work through their own individual reactions. Try, 'Here's what's happening, and we know you're going to have questions. Let's talk about them.'

If you're making an announcement that you know your colleagues will view negatively, the worst thing you can do is try to convince them that it's actually a great thing for them. They will be able to see right through it, and they will view you as insincere and condescending, especially if you stand there and repeat reassuring or soothing phrases over and again. The more often I hear somebody say 'no problem', the more I expect problems.

Where change is likely to impact on the employment or terms and conditions of staff, there is a requirement to consult formally with recognised trade unions as well as the staff involved.

Implementing the change

Once a change is planned, with clear project management procedures, accountability, objectives and timelines in place, it is important to continue with good communication about the rollout and implementation phases.

Change is usually best received when it is implemented in bite sized chunks where at all possible. Most change can be broken down into phases that can be reviewed along the way. Share your implementation timeline with stakeholders.

Review

Change takes time to become established at a school and does not stop when it is introduced. Leaders should continue to stay in close contact with stakeholders and listen to new ideas that may help the change work even better.

However difficult things seem at first, if you have handled matters correctly and maintained integrity, eventually the change will itself become embedded in school culture.

Finance

Finance and accounting; the measurement, processing and communication of financial information. This essential function in a school or MAT is the recording, day-to-day management, strategic leadership and reporting of its finances. Financial planning is an on-going process that assists leaders in making sensible decisions about how to effectively spend money in order to achieve a strategic plan.

A finance procedures manual will be your guidebook, include in it all the essential areas of management, how the processes and procedures run, and who is involved. You might want to include:

- your organisation structure, include the roles and responsibilities of the key finance staff.
- a reference list of the policies that are relevant.
- planning, budgeting and reporting, including budget monitoring, budget controls and accounting reporting.
- auditing and accounting *ie* documentation retention requirements, control account reconciliations, management and statutory accounts.
- income recording and recognition, banking procedures, credit control and debt recovery.
- expenditure processing and recording, ordering processes, wages and salaries, additional payments *ie* mileage claims, trips and visits.
- fixed assets – recognition of assets and depreciation rates.
- investments and reserves.
- equipment and stocks.

- bank account(s) – schedule of signatories, reconciliation procedure, minimum approvals/signatories, charge card details *ie* card holders, transaction limits and card limits.
- taxation *ie* VAT returns, VAT 126.
- insurance.

The key to good financial management is leading and delivering a service to provide the resources needed for the organisation's strategic objectives. It is essential to have a clear set of financial policies and a procedures manual that is followed, and which includes a scheme of delegation that is simple and easy to follow.

Tips for managing finances:

- Regularity of posting *ie* daily, weekly and monthly transactional items, on a timely basis.
- Tracking essential figures, such as pupil number forecasts.
- Reducing the need for manual intervention, for example, moving to cashless systems.
- Removing as far as possible duplication of effort.
- Have segregation of duties and appropriate authorisation, but also not involving too many people.
- Keeping tight and effective control of budgets and spending.
- Being part of influencing the key financial and business decisions, including:
  - o contract management.
  - o growth strategies.
  - o income and fundraising plans.
- Checking for sensibility – does it look right?
- Being a champion of the 3Es – economy, efficiency and effectiveness.
- Ensuring an external independent review for assurance that reports to the board or committee.

Get the financial management software set up correctly from the start, for example a chart of accounts and rates; if you are producing budgets for a number of schools, getting this wrong is going to be costly and time consuming to put right. It is essential to provide sufficient training for the roles and responsibilities of each post holder.

Where possible look for some technological answers that reduce duplication or are more time efficient; bulk data upload, automation and electronic authorisation can all make things easier for you. Create a checklist of month-end tasks that covers the essentials, in addition, having a calendar with key information, for example a schedule of dates when income receipts are due, will assist with cash flow planning

Work to a five-year plan but be aware that it will be largely based on assumptions. Model staffing and 'what if' scenarios to show the impact of possible changes and run them as simulations. For example, the projected impact if the pension contribution percentage increased. Analysing budgets on the concept of current, back two years and forward two years is helpful and it can be useful to compare historical data with current figures to help identify anomalies.

Keep up to date with policy changes, the statutory returns that are required and new initiatives that are launched. Analyse how these changes will impact on your budgets and make all staff aware of financial accountability and what things cost.

Funding

Funding is our key to everything; it dictates our curriculum offer, what we can afford in terms of staffing, how we support children with additional needs, the breadth of extra curricula activities on offer, and almost every other function or operation within the school. The bottom line at the moment is that there is not enough money in the school system and this does not look set to change, but it is an essential part of our role to steer a course safely and profitably through these challenging waters, even if that sometimes means making a sideways turn in order to ultimately keep the whole ship moving forwards.

Many schools are taking tough decisions and are having to narrow what they can offer in some way, but it is always hard to decide what to cut. Reducing the subject options on offer, reducing the number of trips and visits, rethinking the investment in sports, music and the arts, reducing or removing the afterschool clubs, focusing on core subjects. None of these are attractive options and diminish the ability of the school to offer the breadth of learning and experiences that develop the whole child.

The issues surrounding recruitment and retention can become even more difficult in opportunity areas and challenging contexts. These schools often end up with heavy supply staff costs and a high turnover of employed staff. Recruitment, training and temporary cover constitute a significant financial outlay which can increase the burden on other parts of the budget. There are of course other associated problems with an ongoing situation like this; it is difficult to keep consistency of quality in teaching and learning, and supply staff will not always be familiar with the systems and structures of a particular school. This can create and embed further problems that take time and money to rectify.

Financial risk management and security

At a cyber-security conference I attended it was highlighted that we are now more likely to be a victim of a cyber-crime than be burgled, and that it is a matter of when, not if, we are the target, in fact it may have already happened without our knowledge. Fraudsters are targeting businesses with more frequency than individuals because companies with a large cash flow, which includes schools and MATs, will be holding large amounts money in the bank. In this area employees can be our biggest risk. I am not insinuating that employees are perpetrators, I mean that they can be a potential risk. For instance, many people put their emails on to their personal phone or tablet and have the password saved for ease of access, but if they do not have any security, for example a pin number, they are making that information easily accessible to others.

At the event we were given a demonstration of hacking and how easily and quickly information can be accessed without the victim's knowledge that anything is happening. They showed the scenario of someone picking up a memory stick outside of the office environment. It did not have any indication of who it belonged to and the kind person wanted to see if there was information on the stick that would identify the owner so they could return it, after all, it could be important. They inserted it into their computer and from that moment they put the organisation at risk. The fraudster was able to monitor keystrokes, access information not only on that machine but throughout the entire network, and eventually take over the machine. We cannot stop everything, but we can reduce our vulnerability by educating our staff, ensuring they are aware of potential risks and what they can do to minimise them.

If you suspect that you have received a phishing email, do not click links in the emails, use a trusted company website or app to log in. Fraudsters want to be able to harvest information to be able to access money. If you receive a letter or an email notifying you of a change of bank details for a supplier, contact a trusted person at that organisation to check that it is legitimate, many organisations have been caught by this scam.

I am probably telling you things here that you already know, but does everyone in your organisation have the same understanding and knowledge as you?

Top tips:

- Use strong passwords and PIN numbers.
- Stop, think and listen to your instincts.
- Set up auto software updates and use security software.
- Use social media wisely, consider what you share.
- Help to educate others.
- Provide school email accounts for your local governing body members and board directors, reduce the risk of using unsecure email accounts
- If you feel that something is suspicious, discuss it with someone you trust, and if you are a victim of crime, report it.

Tracking figures

Keep a spreadsheet of the budget and outturn figures for a number of years and add in your current year and projections for future years. It is a useful way to track trends in income and expenditure and spot anomalies.

	Year 1		Year 2		Year 3		Year 4
	Budget	Outturn	Budget	Outturn	Budget	Outturn	Forecast
	£	£	£	£	£	£	£
Expenditure:							
Teaching staff							
Supply/agency staff							
Education support staff							
Admin staff							
Premises staff							
Catering staff							
Extended school staff							
Other staff							
Indirect employee expenses							
Premises							
Operating leases							
Insurance							
Supplies and services							
Support costs							
Governance costs							

	Year 1		Year 2		Year 3		Year 4
Total Expenditure							
Income:							
Basic entitlement (AWPU)							
Looked after children (LAC)							
Deprivation							
Prior attainment							
Lump sum							
Minimum funding guarantee							
Education services grant							
Rates							
Government grant income							
Local authority revenue income							
Other income							
Total income							

Budgeting

Working on the budget plan is one of the favourite tasks I get to perform as a business professional, although making the budgets do everything that the schools want to do has become increasingly challenging over the years.

It takes a collective approach between us and the rest of the senior leadership team to come up with more creative solutions, or maybe even going back to zero based budgeting and establishing what the essentials are and what the 'nice to haves' are. As budgets tighten it is important to understand how the figures that drive them work, and the effects that changes will have, for example with regards to the funding formula and modelling changes in the pupil demographic. If you have an increase in the number of children who have additional needs, model how this will impact on your funding; look at what learning support and resources are essential, and what would be nice to have.

Many schools are in a position where budgets are extremely pressured and as such they have to concentrate on the essentials. There have been reports in the press[1] of teachers buying essential resources like books, pens and even food for pupils, in an effort to ensure that their basic needs are met and that they can learn effectively. As business leaders and as schools we are having to be more creative; considering changes to staffing and the way teaching and learning is delivered, collaborating for cost effectiveness and ensuring as far as possible that plans are sustainable. We should all be doing our best to make the budget work for the school.

The best way to prepare financially is:

- to design and implement efficient structures and systems.
- to up-skill and invest in quality professional development that demonstrates impact.
- to continually evaluate the impact of spending and to question whether you are receiving value for money.

Income

Check that projections accurately reflect the demographic *ie* pupil numbers by year group and government initiatives (such as those linked to deprivation and sports, but these change over time). Add in projections for estimated generated income and details for grants brought forward that will be spent in the year.

---

[1]Reference Secret Teacher Buying Supplies (March 2017), The Guardian

Forward plan by estimating any expected movements in pupil numbers and track actual numbers from the termly census returns. For example, you may be a growing school and have increasing numbers moving through, or you might have an unusually small year group. One of the most difficult situations is to be in a school with a falling pupil roll, where you will find it a challenge to meet needs.

I use a spreadsheet which tracks the income expected for each school, split out and allocated to the months that it is expected to be received, and each month I check and agree to the actuals received.

Staffing costs

Check these in detail, line by line:

Hours

Current pay point

Pay ranges

Increments

Back pay entitlement

Pay awards

Secondments

Maternity/paternity/adoption leave

Pension rates

National insurance rates

Temporary hours

Fixed term contracts

Additional payments.

Ideally your total staffing costs as a percentage of income should be 80% or below, if it is higher you run the risk of becoming unsustainable moving forward due to the pressure of rising pay point increments and rising on costs (employer national insurance and pension contributions).

Non-staffing costs

Start with the outturn from the previous year plus inflationary amount and go through line by line. Increase or decrease accordingly areas of one-off spend or additional investment; building maintenance, resources and ICT are common areas. Look at contracts, licences and subscriptions – check if they are all continuing and if there are any price increases anticipated. Analyse the reasons for under or overspends compared to previous budgets.

As an essential part of school life, the cost of ICT should be taken in to account. Schools and MATs will need to have a repair and replacement plan that meets their business, learning and teaching needs. Planning for short and long term requirements, investing in the infrastructure, security and building capacity is all important. We are not talking about one class set of laptops anymore, where half of them do not work. There are more innovative technologies and ways of utilising ITC to best effect and we should be looking at investing in a device per pupil. Investment in complementary learning tools, including 3D printers, green screen and recording technology, virtual reality, coding and robotics will position us well for the future, we need to be proactive not reactive.

Planning for unexpected expenses or price rises can be difficult. I tend to add contingencies where exact figures are not available at the planning stage, for example you may have a capital building project planned and you need to allocate some revenue budgets, without prior expenditure to analyse you can only make a best estimate. Use an inflationary factor on prior year outturn and information provided from specific providers, for instance utility companies often provide advance notice of price rises. If it is not a time pressured expense then look for grant funding that is available.

Reviewing contracts

If you are on a three-month termination period allow a six-month lead in time for any supplies or services that you want to re-tender, prior to the end of the contract. This allows you three months to look at other options, secure quotes, and present your findings to leaders, governors or trustees. When it comes to tendering you can run the procurement process yourself or use a specialist company to do it on your behalf, who will charge either you or the successful supplier.

Month-end checks

Purchase ledger

- Close purchase orders by matching them against invoices and review any outstanding. Check for any that need to be reversed, if for example the order has been cancelled or duplicated in error.
- Process all outstanding purchase invoices and credit notes, then check supplier statements for any that have been missed.
- Check that all documents have been appropriately signed off and authorised.
- Print and check an aged creditors report.
- Highlight any transactions that require further investigation.
- Review the ledger for any transactions that should be recognised as fixed assets.

Sales ledger

- Check that all sales ledger invoices and credit notes have been raised and income matched.
- Send out reminders for overdue accounts.
- Print and check an aged debtors report.
- Highlight any transactions that require further investigation.
- If you use a separate software system for recording daily income, for example for trips and visits, ensure that a reconciliation of the two systems is completed to ensure consistency and accuracy.

Bank accounts and charge cards

Once all the transactions have been processed and entered on the finance system complete the bank and charge card reconciliations. Create a report identifying the unpresented items, and investigating any that require further attention, for example cheques older than six months, which need to be written back.

VAT

Reconcile the VAT, then produce and submit the VAT return or VAT 126 reclaim.

Payroll reconciliation

Check through the payroll thoroughly. If you spot any errors or omissions advise the payroll provider. Checking draft run reports should reduce the number of errors. Complete a month-end reconciliation, clearly identifying the month-end creditors.

Reporting

Once all the transaction processing and reconciliations have been completed, run your month-end reports, including a trail balance, nominal ledger report of all income and expenditure and balance sheet.

Benchmarking

It is important to remember that benchmarking data does not give us the answers, but it does give us a useful starting point for our planning and interventions by highlighting areas which require focus. It is not a tool to use to hold leaders to account, it is a source of financial information.

There are three main ways that I have used benchmarking:

- In schools as part of the annual cycle of financial processes and procedures.
- As a research tool when applying for a position.
- As a due diligence tool as part of a MAT growth strategy.

In schools as part of the annual cycle of financial processes and procedures

By highlighting areas where expenditure is significantly above or below the average, thus identifying possible savings. It is important that it is not just the business manager or finance staff who engage with this data, your senior leadership team and governing board also need to have an awareness and an understanding. In much the same way that I would expect the senior leadership team (including the school business leader) and governing board to be engaging with pupil performance and progress data. It is good practice to offer a session each year for any of the governors who want to go through the information in detail.

As a research tool when applying for a position

When I decided to apply for the position of finance director, part of my due diligence was to look at their data. It is a really easy way to prepare for a professional interview. The information is publicly available and can give you a flavour of their income and expenditure. If you are asked what you know about the organisation's income stream, you could refer to the data to say, for example 'I can see from your data that you are generating rental income and I think you could increase that income by linking with local sports clubs'. It demonstrates that you already understand something about how the organisation runs.

As a due diligence tool as part of the MAT growth strategy

As we look to potentially grow our multi-academy trust, benchmarking is an essential tool for use as part of the due diligence process.

Metric tool

The Department for Education's metric tool takes your school and groups it with 49 others to give you an indication of your school's efficiency based on pupil attainment and the money the school receives for pupils, it also ranks that list. This can give you a different data set to use for gathering information. If you are not near the top of the list you can initiate research to discover what higher ranked schools are doing that could be used in your setting. The benchmarking and metric tool are available free from the Department for Education.

Next steps

Benchmarking is useful as an indicator, but what I found more helpful as a school business manager was working with a peer group to get behind the data in to a more detailed analysis.

A small group of school business managers from a similar area, with a similar demographic can get together and look at detailed information. For example, how much you pay for a ream of paper, how much you pay for energy, how you deal with staffing absence and PPA cover, what your staffing structure looks like, or what your business support staff structure looks like. This is something I would really encourage you to think about doing. I believe that collaboration is the way forward, we are not always in competition with each other and we need to work together to improve outcomes for all our pupils.

Kreston Reeves produce an annual 'Academies Benchmark Report' which you can sign up to receive for free, it is a useful document to read and share with your SLT, governors and finance colleagues.

View from an expert

The joy of benchmarking – Emma Gray, finance director, Cotswold Beacon Academy Trust

The problem is not the problem; the problem is your attitude about the problem.

Jack Sparrow

It's taken me 15 years, and a life lesson from a Disney character, to realise that my dislike of benchmarking has been entirely down to my own attitude and approach.

Back in my early days as an SBM, I was keen to impress governors (and follow DfE advice) by taking a benchmarking item along to every finance committee meeting. For years, I took one of four subjects; income, expenditure, staffing or utilities and benchmarked against my own school's year-on-year trend, local schools of similar size and the DfE's national benchmarking data. It usually took me a day to gather the information together and present it in bar charts and narrative that I hoped the governors would find interesting. If they found time to look at it at all, it was, at best, a cursory glance and I became more and more frustrated and disillusioned with the process.

Eventually the chair of finance took me to one side; 'We know you well enough by now, Emma, that if you had concerns about any of these topics, you'd flag it long before its turn on the benchmarking calendar. Tell us something we don't know.' So I put benchmarking down for a while and focused on improving my monthly management information so that it would automatically flag if there was an issue with any of those four subjects.

Recently though, my interest in benchmarking has been revived as I've been thinking about how I can use it positively, not only for improving efficiencies, but also for the wellbeing of staff:

- Is there a correlation between how many biscuits we buy and staff happiness? Both are easily measurable. If this was proven to be true, would buying more biscuits make staff happier? And how many biscuits do other schools buy?

- How does our grounds keeping spend compare to that of other schools? Would spending more money on school grounds, and planting in particular, improve the wellbeing of students and staff or would it just get trampled with the football?

- How does our school environment make stakeholders feel and do they appreciate our efforts with litter picking, recycling and eco-friendliness?

- When we are having a drive on energy-efficiency and 'environmental justice' (as our students like to call it) does our energy use actually go up or down?

- What do other schools pay for paper? Is there a way of driving the price of paper down further, and when we believe that we have found the optimal price (we have a team member who drives a very hard bargain) can we find a way to share this price with other schools?

What I have finally realised is that benchmarking doesn't have to be dull. Make the monitoring of routine subjects something that you do as a matter of course and report this to governors if there is an issue. Then find topics that interest you and share these with them because, most of all, they want to see passion and motivation from their SBM.

Reporting

My main aims when producing a financial report:

- To ensure that it is easy to read and understandable, for an audience of finance and non-finance experienced leaders, governors and/or trustees.
- Ensuring that it has a flow, with key headings and sections, making it easy for the reader to understand.
- Highlight the key information of which the reader needs to be aware, including achievements, progress, improvements, issues, concerns, pressures and assumptions made in forecasting, along with actions taken and next steps, all kept as succinct as possible.
- Cover the areas expected, a report for governors may include finance, HR, H&S, building and facilities, ICT, marketing, PR and training, depending on your committee and agenda structure, and your roles and responsibilities.

Reporting using the ten questions for governors

This example takes the school information and local or national averages as comparators, using the information to demonstrate to leaders of governance that the school is spending and providing value in line with other organisations. It is a way of benchmarking on key areas:

- Staff pay as a percentage of total expenditure
- Average teacher costs
- Pupil to teacher ratio
- Class sizes
- Teacher contact ratio
- Proportion of budget spent on the leadership team
- Three to five-year budget projections
- Spend per pupil on expenditure lines compared to similar schools
- School improvement plan priorities and the relative cost options
- List of contracts with costs and renewal dates

Reporting on business improvement priorities

This example is more akin to a school improvement reporting structure, whereby for example, the school may be working on financial efficiency or cost saving measures, or a recovery or improvement plan. This structure would demonstrate progress against the specific actions identified:

- Priority 1
  - o Outline of the priority
  - o Action plan targets – with a progress report on stage of completion and whether it is on track *ie* not started, superseded, part-completed, completed
  - o Impact statement
  - o Current issues
  - o Next steps

Income generation

Fundraising strategy

A fundraising strategy does not have to take up a lot of time and it does not need to be a complex plan. Using a couple of hours to decide what to focus on will be time well spent in the long run. Your aim is to maximise the opportunities available to you with the minimal amount of effort and cost. Ideally this would be best done as a team, because most things are easier when you can share the workload. It could be as simple as a one page diagram which summarises the key points.

The basic components for your plan are:

- vision and goals
- projects
- people
- knowledge and expertise
- marketing

Outline a vision of what you want to achieve. Set the goals for your fundraising strategy and make them in to SMART targets. A key point to establish has to be your target, how much do you want to raise? What will the impact be if achieved? What are you already doing? Is it successful?

Draft a project narrative that outlines what you want to achieve in the short, medium and long term. Will it impact on pupil attainment and progress? Will it impact a specific group, or does it have a wider reach?

Include the specifics of – where, when, how, what, who and why. The 'Why' is essential when it comes to marketing and meeting the criteria of grant funding organisations

Include the following key points in your project narrative:

- Title
- Description
- Why you need the project
- What the expected impact of the project is
- References to evidence that the project will support the targeted need

For instance, you might be looking to fundraise for a market garden project as part of an enrichment activity and to improve children's understanding of healthy eating by growing and cooking with fresh home-grown ingredients; a project that will see pupils and community members working together, in a dedicated space, year on year. You can easily see how this can be presented in a positive light; it is a long term sustainable project, it is aimed at healthy living and will have impact on current and future pupils, as well as the local community.

Grant giving organisations are interested in projects that will have a direct impact on the wellbeing of children and young people, with sustainability also being an important factor. Is this project a one off? The ideal project will be sustainable and build on positive outcomes for children (current and future), their families and the wider community. Include details of groups that will be able to use the project, for example sports groups, weekend clubs, and local families.

Engage your existing supporters and stakeholders, including staff, pupils, PTA, and local businesses. Create a database of the companies that you have links with, such as suppliers where family members of pupils and staff work. Compile a database of grant funding, keep a track of those applications which were successful and those which were not. If it is knowledge or expertise that you need, identify what you require and who could supply it.

Think about what you need and how it will be used, is it money, time, people, resources? For instance, I recently shared a post on social media from an SBM friend who was looking for an old rowing boat to upcycle in to a children's sandpit.

Identify the best and most relevant marketing routes and media channels available to maximise your coverage and target the right audience. Social media is brilliant for raising the profile of fundraising projects, especially they involve staff and pupils. Awareness can grow exponentially incredibly swiftly, promoting the cause to wider networks and increasing the likelihood of donations.

Maximise your available resources, walk around your school site and look at what is not being used effectively, include the sports hall, gym, swimming pool, equipment storage and playing fields, and don't forget the staff, they could well be your most valuable resource. Think beyond the school day.

There are many ways to raise money and obtain physical resources and time:

- Applying for grants
- Crowd funding
- Business sponsorship

- Leases and lettings
- Incentivisation schemes
- Volunteers and parent helpers
- Alumni
- Pupil-led initiatives
- Parent and carer skills audit
- Fashion show
- Treasure hunt
- Fun day
- Talent show
- Art and photo exhibition
- Festival – arts, music, food
- Murder mystery nights
- Pamper evenings
- Swishing event
- Clubs and activities for adults or children – sports, crafts, arts, music, yoga, pilates, dance classes
- Family photographs
- Book of stories or poems
- Tea towels
- Bake sale
- Competitions
- Car boot sales
- Craft market
- Ball
- Auction
- Quiz night
- Disco

Crowdfunding

Crowdfunding is a quick and easy way of raising funds, via a larger number of small donations, usually via an online platform. So rather than asking one person or organisation for a one off donation for a project or initiative, each individual makes a small contribution. You can target a wide stakeholder audience by using crowdfunding. In school communities we already have a network of support from groups and individuals such as pupils, ex-pupils, parents and carers, grandparents, local businesses and public figures, all of whom can be targeted.

If you were to invest time in securing a single donation of £1,000.00 it would take time to research and secure a potential donor, investing significant time and effort in the process. Whereas via a crowd funding campaign you could ask a 1,000 people to donate £1 each, it can be quick and easy. If people buy-in to what you are raising the funds for, if they can understand the benefit the project will have, you may raise much more that you need.

Tips for using crowdfunding:

- Firstly, decide upon a project team and create a detailed project plan. The funding is only one element.

- Focus on one project at a time and be clear about the vision, aims and outcomes for it. Try and make it something different or innovative that will capture people's hearts and minds.

- Make sure that you have a compelling and engaging story that will bring an emotional connection between the project and donors.

- Outline the time frame, remember to avoid other peak times for fundraising like Children in Need or Comic Relief or when there are other financial pressures such as religious celebrations.

- Use good quality photos, if you don't have one, think about investing in a good quality DSLR camera, or see if you can borrow one.

- Create a marketing database and use it well.

- Promote everything through social media, the local press, the school newsletter, and school messaging facilities.

- Keep people updated with the fundraising total and try to build momentum. Don't forget to add in any donations that are received through other methods.

- Create a video – make it a class project.

- Keep saying thank you and think about what incentive or reward you will give your donors, what about a handwritten note from a pupil, or a card designed by ICT or art students? But think in advance about how many you might need, if you attract 500 separate donations, that's a lot of time, paper, card, ink and postage. It might be better to create a poster with a list of donors for display in the school.

Grant applications

There are approximately 7,000 grant making trusts and foundations in the UK.

The key to being successful with grants is aligning your vision with that of the funding bodies and making sure that you write what they need to know on the application form.

If you are looking to apply for grants for a specific project, write an outline of the vision. This means that when you spot a possible grant you already have all the key information to hand. This will save a lot of time if you are applying for multiple grants from different sources.

Your vision document should contain essentially the same information that will be required during the grant application process.

Goals

Set out your goals in terms of what you want to achieve in the short, medium and long term:

- What you want to achieve in 12 months.
- What you want to achieve in 2-5 years.
- What you want to achieve in 5+ years.

Be clear on what projects or activities you want to fund. Test yourself on what you have outlined and why. For example, a key question is to ask why the school cannot fund the project. Why do you need to have the support of an external grant provider?

Funding bodies will want to maximise the impact of the money they donate. Describe how the funding will impact positively of the lives of young people at your school and ideally the wider community.

Project plan

Write a clear project plan and include the following elements:

Title

Think of a relevant and catchy title that succinctly describes the project in as few words as possible.

Description

Outline in the project in more detail. How will the funds be spent? Have specifications, quotes and detailed costings prepared. Who is it going to help?

Can you go wider than pupils at your school alone? Will it help other schools, childcare providers, sports clubs and/or local groups?

Why

Why do you need the project? 'Because the Headteacher wants it' is not a good answer, here is a better example:

> We would like to purchase a set of 35 ICT devices, that can be utilised by all pupils as part of delivering a cross curricula approach to all subjects that is enhanced by the use of technology. This will provide our young people with skills for the future and allow them to experience technology in a safe environment. It is an essential part of the school's vision that our pupils leave with the best possible start to the rest of their lives, and that means providing a holistic approach that nurtures and develops the child as a whole.

Impact

What impact will it have if you are able to buy these resources? How many lives will it impact and in what way? Why is it important? What will be different? If you are asking for part funding for a project, how will you fundraise the difference?

Evidence

This is where research and national strategies are important. Use published statistics to support your bid. What evidence can you provide about your intended impacts? Provide evidence of how a similar project or use of equipment has been demonstrably proven to improve outcomes in similar settings. How are you going to know and demonstrate that it has been a success – is the outcome measurable?

Business sponsorship

Can businesses be the perfect partners?

I believe that the right companies can make perfect partners and can add value and enrich children's learning and life experiences. Business sponsorship comes in many forms including the donation of cash, products, services and time. Larger organisations have a commitment to giving to worthy causes through Corporate Social Responsibility (CSR), although often these details are not easy to find.

Donations might consist of a one-off pledge, for example a prize for the school fayre, time volunteering during careers week or enterprise events, delivery of an assembly, or an on-going relationship such as paying to have an advert in the school newsletter.

An easy way to get started with business sponsorship is to review the companies that you have spent money with over the last 12 months and list them in order of the highest spend.

Pick the top five to ten companies and make a list of their name, your key contact, contact details and what products or services they supply. Now think about what you would like to get from the partnership and have a clear understanding of what you would be able to offer in return, taking in to consideration whether they will be your sole provider for a set period of time, and what you are able to promote in terms of the use of branding.

Always think carefully about whether the partnership has any potential to cause reputational damage to your organisation.

Further steps

- Scan through local newspapers and magazines to find companies that have previously supported schools or charities.
- Make a list of the big employers in your area and who in the organisation would be the best person to contact.
- Most supermarkets offer an opportunity for projects from local schools to be nominated with the possibility of winning small grants.
- Make contact with the local chamber of commerce and business networking groups.

Incentives

Use incentives to maximise funding streams. A small incentive can help to increase the take-up of an offer. For example, at the time of writing additional funding is available through the Pupil Premium Grant for pupils who are or have been entitled to free school meals. The registration of each eligible pupil brings in much needed funding to support children from disadvantaged backgrounds. Offering parents and carers a small incentive to complete the required paperwork can sometimes be all the persuasion that families need. This needs to be thought about and handled very sensitively, it is essential not to single out families by only approaching those you think maybe entitled. Have forms to hand at school events, such as the reception parents' welcome meetings, offer an incentive, such as a free water bottle or age appropriate reading book for completing the form. The return on investment is well worth it.

Alumni

I recently read a wonderful report in a local publication of how Nick Jenkins, of Dragon's Den fame had supported his childhood school. Nick Jenkins successfully launched and grew the online greetings card company moonpig. com, which was reportedly sold in 2011 for an estimated £120million. It was reported in the article that he went to his old school offering help to and advice to pupils, presented a lecture, met young enterprise groups and launched a Dragon's Den styled project with one year group. Think how amazing it would be to have the opportunity to give pupils that sort of mentoring opportunity, with pupils picking up advice for the future from one of the country's leading entrepreneurs.

Not every school has an ex-pupil who has gone on to become a TV or movie star, a sports hero or a millionaire, but you may well have a whole host of people who are successful in all sorts of personal and professional fields. You might find that you have a well-known scientist, author, or even headteacher listed among your old students. Those with fond memories of their time at school will often want to give back in some way.

Start by asking your local staff if there are any ex-pupils who they know of who have gone on to achieve something special, personal experiences and networks can be powerful.

Pupil-led initiatives

A school in Birmingham recently won a national award in the category of 'Financial/fundraising initiative of the year' and it is easy to see why. Their project is reported to have raised £35,000 in six days and was focused on a group of students working as a team and utilising their individual skills to greatest effect. Their activities included using debating team members to phone alumni, student artists designing a new logo, technology enthusiasts working on social media content and drama students helping to film a video campaign. I can imagine the great enthusiasm and energy that would have come from pupils working together with the aim of raising funds for the school. This sort of venture would provide brilliant learning experiences that give a real-life perspective and enable pupils to develop skills for the future.

Parent and carer skills audit

I picked up a brilliant idea recently from my daughter's schools. During parents' evening there is often time when parents and carers are waiting, the school decided to make use of this time by handing out a parent and carer skills audit questionnaire. I have often thought that it would be a useful idea to build a database of the professions or trades of parents and carers, but this idea took it further to include skills that come from personal interests as well as professional ones.

The form they used was simple, it set out the types of skills and interests they were looking for and stated that it was part of their commitment to strengthening links between the school and the community.

It also included the following:

- Contact details
- Skills, interests and hobbies:
  - Fundraising
  - Marketing
  - Gardening
  - Social media
  - Languages
  - Music
  - Art and design
  - Photography
  - Books
  - Dance
  - Cooking
  - Sculpture
  - Pottery
  - Writing
  - Travel
  - Science
  - Drama
  - Textiles
  - Maths
  - ICT
  - Sport
  - Environment
  - Health and fitness

- o Culture
- o Other
- What time could you offer, for example every week, once per half term, weekends, as and when, and other.
- Contacts that you have with local companies.
- Community groups that you are linked with.
- Friends or relatives who would be useful links for the school.

Take in to account that we need to comply with general data protection regulations (GDPR) in having consent for the information we have and how we will use it. I would add a specific section at the end about consent and use of the information and ask for a signature and date.

Top tip

Do not put all your hopes and aspirations in to a single type of income generation. Spread the risk and effort and give yourself options. It is likely that this will be an additional task on top of an already heavy workload, so plan, share and spread the work over time.

Marketing and Public Relations

The science and art of exploring, creating and delivering value to satisfy the needs of a target market at a profit. Marketing identifies unfulfilled needs and desires. It defines, measures and quantifies the size of the identified market and potential profit.

Dr Philip Kotler

Marketing

There are three important ideas to consider in building your marketing strategy and a respected brand:

- Decisions are based on emotions.
- Colour, and how you use it, is important.
- Images are processed faster than words.

Decisions are based on emotions

When you are marketing your school, you are selling parents and carers a vision of their child's future. Showing them what their child could achieve, what they could experience, what the future could hold for them if they choose your school.

If your school hosts an annual open day, what is the customer experience like? Do you focus on the children or the adults? How does you school look, smell and feel? Make sure the displays are neat, that the school is clean and smells nice, and that the temperature is pleasant.

Remember, you are selling your school to the children as well as the adults, include elements for everyone. Ensure that staff on hand are helpful and pleasant. Little things make a big difference, such as having someone on parking duty and having something that they takeaway, perhaps a goody bag.

My daughter's school give every child that starts the school a book bag, a water bottle and a sunhat. All the items have the school logo on and are personalised with the pupil's name. This is something that the parents' association fund each year and I thought it was a lovely gesture, it mattered to me that someone had taken the time to do this.

Colour and how you use it is important

It is recognised that we identify certain qualities and meanings with certain colours:

- Blue is the colour of trust, loyalty and intelligence. It is used by companies like Facebook, Twitter, Ford, Nasa, Dell and OralB.
- Red is the colour for strength, excitement and potential danger. It is used by companies like Coca Cola, Kelloggs, Lego and Canon; and for things like Health and Safety signage.
- Yellow is recognised as being a colour that shows intellect, joy and intelligence. It is used by companies like AA, Nikon, McDonalds and National Geographic.
- Green is associated with freshness, growth and safety. It is used by companies like Waitrose, Land Rover and BP; and for things like First Aid points.

Use the same logo and colours across all your communication and media tools including your uniform, website, letterhead, social media, press releases and school brochure or prospectus.

Images are processed faster than words.

We all know the term 'a picture paints a thousand words.' Images are one of your greatest marketing tools. Create powerful visuals that demonstrate your school's core values and curriculum offering. I once visited a school which had some fantastic art work on display, they had large canvas prints of inspirational people. One was of Malala Yousafzai, accompanied by the words 'I am stronger than fear'. It was a powerful image that has stuck in my mind.

View from an expert

How do you market your school? – Andy Heron FISBL, school business manager

In the past, marketing a school would have seen organisations expending effort and expenditure on the following items:

- School prospectus
- School newsletters
- Parents evenings
- Open evenings
- Letters to parents
- Press articles

Many of these would have been in paper form and posted out to everyone and anyone with the intention of providing information about the school and to convey the school's ethos, message and brand in order to ensure that sufficient interest was gained to provide adequate pupil numbers in any given year.

Latterly, while some of the above list are still relevant and bear fruit in terms of generating interest from a local catchment area, it is in the digital world where school marketing really comes to the fore. We can look at the following when considering where school information and reputation is viewed:

- School website
- School Facebook page
- School twitter feed
- Online school payment systems – such as Parentpay
- Inspection reports

Marketing though, to me, is much more than just what is listed above. It can be considered to include the following important areas:

- PR/media management
- Branding
- Event management

- Print and design management
- Email, web and telephone communications
- Social media
- Reputation management
- Stakeholder management
- Market research
- Fundraising

Social media alone in its variety of sources gives the school multiple opportunities to convey the marketing and branding of the school on a global scale which can be viewed anywhere in the world. In many schools departments have their own twitter feeds to communicate to followers what is happening in the world of, for instance art, geography or politics.

Spreading the school message far and wide

Stakeholders are able to readily access this information at any time, giving your work immediate prominence an allowing it to be evaluated and absorbed.

What is vital to all types of school marketing, be they traditional or digital is the methodology and strategy that is employed when deciding on which method is best for your school.

I recall from my DSBM studies looking at Nicholas Foskett and his views on stakeholder involvement being a key attribute to ensuring that marketing was being achieved in the right way.

> *Such an organisational refocusing in schools brings an important cultural challenge, yet, in many dimensions, is not far removed from the traditional operating approach of 'good' schools, with their focus on comprehensiveness, community and partnership with stakeholders.*

> (Foskett, 1998)

To that end, marketing strategy could be viewed as a cycle – it is a never-ending process and continually moving as both technology and stakeholders change.

When thinking about your marketing strategy and how it will look and work, you might want to consider the following:

- Market research – interviewing and surveying current and prospective parents and analysing the findings.

- Meeting market needs – for example, you could consider what your school does to meet the needs of prospective parents, and what it could do.

- Message and brand development – identifying three or four key statements about the school and a simple visual design for the website.

- Evidence gathering – regularly collecting news stories about the school that support your key messages.

- Using mass media – the stories gathered in the previous stage can be communicated to the local community through posters, social media and publications.

- Relationship management – keeping in touch with anyone who has shown interest in the school, whether they have attended an event, asked for a prospectus or spoken to a member of staff.

There are many models which are freely available for your use, the following are just a few examples that can be used to identify areas for exploration. While not specifically aimed at education establishments it is often helpful to see what else can and should be considered.

The 7Ps approach, an intricate model to use that is more aligned to product marketing but has some useful topics to consider.

The 4Ps approach, getting these four boxes all ticked would mean getting the mix right, although price is more the price of the product item rather than budgetary cost. A prospectus run for example, or an advert for an open evening.

Marketing your school will often be an individualised task and what works for one school or MAT may not work for another. However, in carrying out a review of the marketing strategy, any omissions or areas of weakness should be identified.

Marketing can be a very involved aspect of the SBM role and as usual with most things it is often the identification of what you want to achieve that will determine the time that is required to produce the results that you want. Listing your goals and what you want to achieve or can often be the

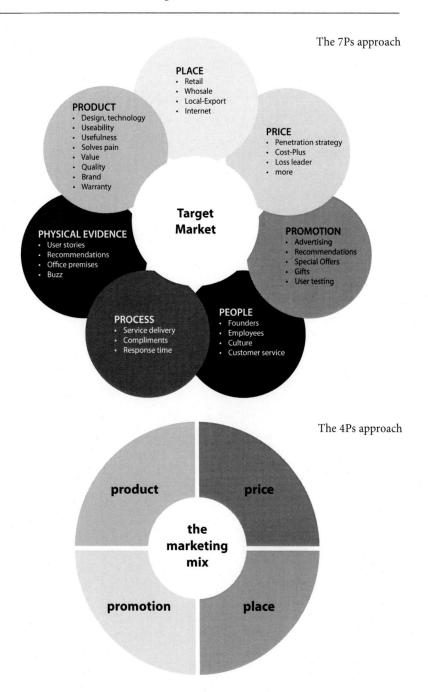

The 7Ps approach

PLACE
- Retail
- Whosale
- Local-Export
- Internet

PRODUCT
- Design, technology
- Useability
- Usefulness
- Solves pain
- Value
- Quality
- Brand
- Warranty

PRICE
- Penetration strategy
- Cost-Plus
- Loss leader
- more

Target Market

PHYSICAL EVIDENCE
- User stories
- Recommendations
- Office premises
- Buzz

PROMOTION
- Advertising
- Recommendations
- Special Offers
- Gifts
- User testing

PROCESS
- Service delivery
- Compliments
- Response time

PEOPLE
- Founders
- Employees
- Culture
- Customer service

The 4Ps approach

product

price

the marketing mix

promotion

place

place to start, but always key is ensuring that these aims are measurable so that you can determine whether or not they have been successful during this phase of your marketing plan or cycle. Think carefully about your desired outcomes:

- Raising awareness
- Enhancing reputation
- Building credibility in a specialism
- Recruiting pupils
- Retaining staff
- Raising funds

But remember one thing about your project; even miracles take a little time.

References

Foskett, N. (1998) Schools and Marketization, Cultural Challenges and Responses. *Educational Management Administration & Leadership* 26 (2) pp. 197-210.

Building a brand

Branding

- Name
- Logo
- Identity
- Marketing
- Strategy
- Colours

A brand is a name, design, symbol, logo or distinguishing feature that is used in business, marketing and advertising and which is associated with a product or service. Brand management is the application of marketing techniques to maximise the positive perception, visibility, reach and impact of a brand in order to increase awareness and uptake. Branding and marketing is used to build awareness and a desired perception, encouraging customers to be loyal and trust in the company. Advertising is used to attract new customers and keep existing ones, and to exert influence and control over their purchase decisions, making you believe that you need to buy in to that brand and what they stand for. Companies like Apple excel at this and have created the most incredible brand loyalty.

Often a recognisable symbol is used in the business or organisation's logo, usually the designs are simple but bold, for example the apple used by Apple Computers and the tick used by Nike.

Be consistent in your school or MAT branding. Ensure that all advertising channels are up to date, including the school website and social media pages. First impressions can make or break a decision. Is the 'latest news' or 'update' section still giving information about the school being closed due to snow even though it is now the middle of May? Are you working in partnership with other providers, either formally or informally? Are you telling your potential customers everything they need to know? Does it have everything you would expect as a parent or carer? Is your offer clear? The more transparent you are, the easier and simpler your customers' journey becomes, the more positive the perception of your school will be, making it less likely that negative issues will arise. Think about the little details, for example what about your email address, is your brand name in the address? Is it as short as possible?

Top tips

Be consistent in your branding. Pull together business cards, letterheads, invoices, letters, brochures, websites, adverts, uniforms and signage under one brand umbrella. Put as much time, thought and attention to detail into your social media strategy, as you would when printing something on to your school newsletter, proofread everything thoroughly and ensure that there are no spelling or grammatical errors.

View from an expert

Marketing your school – Justin Smith MInstF, owner, Chameleon Training and Consultancy

'It's all a bit fluffy isn't it, that marketing lark. Airy fairy stuff, and to be honest I don't have time for it.'

So, said a delegate before walking into one my school marketing workshops a while ago. And to be fair, she was an overworked SBM juggling more plates than a circus performer, with her mind on the chaos she was likely to walk into when returning to school. And you can't blame anyone for their suspicion of the value of school marketing, after all, if you're not measuring it, how can you place a value on it?

But firstly, what do we actually mean by 'marketing' in the context of education? There are many definitions, but perhaps my favourite was first given by Davis and Ellison in 1997; 'the means by which the school actively communicates and promotes its purpose, values and products to the pupils, parents, staff and wider community'. There are two key words here; purpose and values. Do you really understand those of your school?

We don't want our schools run like corporate businesses and understandably there may be a negative, dismissive response to discussions around core values, purpose, branding, key messages and the like. But we do operate in a people centric industry – people lie at the heart of what we do; we're about relationships and emotive responses. Successful organisations, with instantly recognisable brands, have built a loyal consumer base because they develop long term, sustainable relationships with their customers. Marketing your school so it builds upon its reputation, or begins to modify a damaged reputation, is the most effective way to secure positive and willing engagement with parents, community and potential investors.

Benjamin Franklin, one of the founding fathers of the United States, claimed 'It takes many good deeds to build a good reputation, and only one bad one to lose it.' Reputation is synonymous with success, there are many factors which can influence parental decision making when it comes to choosing a school for their children, but the reputation, respect and credibility afforded by the school brand plays a significant part. So, invest time to talk with staff, students and parents – understand what makes your school unique, articulate those core values, develop those key messages and make sure they are communicated clearly in everything you do.

It was Theodore Roosevelt who said, 'Nobody cares how much you know, until they know how much you care'. I love this quotation and when it comes to defining your marketing strategies and positioning your school, this should sit at the heart of how you think and what you do. Some of us operate in primary schools in isolated rural communities, others within huge MATs in urban conglomerations, but we share the same commitment to do the best we can for our pupils. It's easy to lose sight of this when labouring over strategic approaches to income generation or devising cunning new ways to engage on social media.

Perhaps we should start with another question: does marketing matter? If a school's purpose is to educate children and young people, does it really matter if it articulates its purpose and values effectively? None of us has a crystal ball, we can't predict the future and we have no idea how the education landscape may look, in for instance 2030. But, ask yourself the question – over the next decade can you really see a situation where our schools, flush with cash and government investment, operate in an uncompetitive, stress free environment? No, me neither.

Marketing your school isn't a single activity or event. It's a structured and coherent process, backed by market research and underpinned by a clear vision of what you're trying to achieve. Reacting spontaneously can be time-consuming and ineffective, and you're unlikely to make a successful case for money to support your promotional campaigns if you don't know what works and why. It makes sense to approach marketing holistically, and I often ask schools to do their thinking away from the busy office. Summer holiday time away from school is ideal – use it to unclutter your mind and think differently. Many may be resistant to the concept of marketing (the name alone conjures up images of corporate business) but meeting the challenges of competition, recruitment, retention, and tighter budgets requires a different mind-set.

There is a tangible relationship between marketing and income generation. If you're able to position yourself attractively, and highlight your key messages and values, then you're more likely to attract new investment. Aligning yourselves with partners and sponsors who share your vision can be extremely beneficial. Remember, it isn't always about hard cash and transactional relationships with business. Alliances with strategic partners can bring about mutual benefits.

Your marketing and communications strategy can enable interaction with former students who are only too willing to get involved in school projects, giving their time and knowledge and sharing their experiences with younger generations.

Additionally, with over £1 billion donated to UK universities in 2017 by former students, there should be no reason for schools to shy away from asking for their share of the pie. Independent schools are very adept and experienced at running legacy campaigns, raising over £130 million annually in donations – it's time for the state sector to sharpen their marketing messages to this audience and muscle in on the action.

At my last school, I established a cricket academy for our Year 7 and Year 8 pupils, funded by former students. The initiative was attractive to external funders who acknowledged the self-funding aspect underpinning future sustainability; Sport England pledged funds to support the project and a wider campaign to fund a multi-sport pavilion at the school was launched. Marketing your ambitions to alumni can kick-start similar projects. Oh, and the lady I mentioned at the beginning – well, she's now a happy marketing convert, and I have no doubt she'll be putting the finishing touches to her school marketing plan over the summer holidays.

References

Davies, B. and Ellison, L. (1997) *School leadership for the 21st century*. London: Routledge.

Build your personal brand

There are two types of people in life; those who use themselves to benefit others and those who use others to benefit themselves.

I know lots of SBMs who are firmly in category one, including all the amazing people who have collaborated with me to publish this book. I believe that we earn our place in life by being hardworking, honest and loyal, it is not something to which we are entitled.

When I think about branding, I think about popularity and that is a concept I am not completely comfortable with. When I was at school for instance, it was not possible to be popular without wearing Adidas 3-Stripe jogging bottoms! If one professional is popular, does it make others unpopular? I have always been happy accepting that I am different, and I do not feel a need to follow the crowd.

I see value in building powerful personal professional brands that support future opportunities and increase awareness and understanding of the profession and the ongoing improvements in the sector. This is not achieved by listening to one or two voices recognised as being popular, it comes from sharing practice and knowledge from as many professionals as possible and being part of a collective professional voice.

I want to see every SBM being proud of who they are and what they are good at, and celebrating their unique brand.

Top tip

Have a professional photo taken and use it across all your professional media platforms.

Share your story

Whether we like it or not, we already have a brand. People are already making a judgement about who we are and what we stand for. I think we fear the judgement of others, I have had so many conversations with parents on the playground recently about the accepted protocol for children's parties! I give a similar response each time, something along the lines of, as a parent I do what I think is right for my child. If she asked to have two friends to a party at the ice rink, rather than inviting the whole class to a disco party, that is what I would organise. I try to be a parent who does what is right for their child, not what I think another parent will expect from me. The message I am sharing here is be clear about what your story as an individual is and what you stand for, whether it be at work or at home. Be happy with living who you are every day, be deliberate in the way you walk, talk, communicate and essentially live. Be who you want to be and be consistent in how you share that message. Do and say what you believe to be the right thing.

Be self-aware

Be self-aware of your reputation, ask your friends, peers and colleagues what it is like to be around you and what they think of you. In the past I have done a 360-degree review, which included a self-assessment of my personality type, identifying those areas in which I felt I was strong, and then asking a number of colleagues for feedback on my findings. What did they think I was good at? Where could I improve? I chose colleagues that I had complete trust in and asked them to be as honest as possible. The feedback helped me to change the way I interacted with my team and increased my self-awareness.

To develop a sense of what your personal brand could be like, consider the following questions, and do not restrict yourself to thinking about your current work role, that is only one element of your life:

- What do you do better than others?
- What advice do people come to you for (list your top three)?
- What are your unique skills, knowledge and experiences (list your top three)?
- What are you passionate about (list your top three)?
- What are your values? What really matters to you?

These answers are the start of defining and refining your brand. Try to deliver a consistent message and an authoritative voice that reinforces your competence in these areas.

Top tips:

- Define who you are and what you what to be known for in the education sector.
- Be consistent and authentic.
- Use social media to your advantage. It is not necessary to have thousands of followers or connections. My best learning comes from a small group of professionals that I regularly connect and interact with.
- Engage with others. Be interesting. Be passionate.
- Quality over quantity, always proofread anything that you publish.

Communication map

In schools, we are awash with information that needs to be distributed to the right people at the right time, and we have various methods at our fingertips with which to send it. Stakeholder engagement is important; how and when we communicate information can influence the level of engagement.

Think about your communication methods, the information that you want to distribute and who you want it to reach. Be clear with your stakeholders concerning how and when they will receive information.

Have you thought about what information you communicate through which media types?

Are you doubling or tripling up by sharing information on every available platform?

Think about your communication strategy. Start by drawing a spider diagram of the types of communication methods you are using:

> **Communication mapping**
>
> - Website
> - Social media/app
> - Letters
> - Newsletter
> - Notice boards/electronic display
> - Messaging - email/text

Next, make a list of what information you distribute, the methods you use for this, the frequency of publication and who you are aiming to reach:

Communication media type	Information distributed	Update frequency	Audience
Website	Statutory requirements	Daily/weekly	
	Class/group/club pages		
	Live newsfeed		
	Social media live feed		
	Newsletters		
	Key staff information		
	Contact information		
	School meal menu		

Communication media type	Information distributed	Update frequency	Audience
Social media/ school app	Reminders Live updates School Calendar	Daily during term time	
Letters (paper/ electronic)	Trips and visits information Persmission slips	*Ad hoc*	
Newsletter (paper/ electronic)	Key dates Message from the headteacher Club/events news Class attendance	Weekly/half-termly/ termly	
Messaging (email/ text)	Urgent/vital	*Ad hoc* during school hours	

Finally go back through the list and rationalise whether you have considered the following:

- Do you have parents and carers who are not able to read?
- Do you have parents and carers who speak little English?
- Do you have children that live between two homes?
- Do you have parents and carers with learning needs, who for example need information printed on specific coloured paper so that they can read it?
- What about those children who are persistently absent, is the information getting home?
- If you are aiming to get an award like Schools Games Mark or Eco Schools Award, do you need to embrace social media?
- Do potential business sponsorship organisations or partners know you exist?
- Are you utilising a social media post planner to reach your target audience?

For a communication strategy to be successful, it is fundamental that information is accurate and getting to those who need it, when they need it, in a form they can access and understand. Above all be clear with your stakeholders concerning how and when they will receive information.

Staff news

Create a weekly newsletter for all staff. Be brave and ban using whole school email shots, because we get too many emails as it is. Consider the best way to distribute the newsletter for your setting, for instance if you have a TV screen in your staff room, create your own news channel. It is easy to do, create a PowerPoint presentation containing all the information and run it on a loop.

Make your newsletter fun and engaging. Reduce the email overload by pulling together all the information that you need staff to read in to one place. Include news, updates, HR information, CPD opportunities, planned works such as IT and building work, teaching and learning resources, key dates, fundraisers, H&S updates, safeguarding reminders, thank you messages, and maybe positive pictures and quotes.

Share activities and news, use it to break down the barriers that can build up from working in departments and having a large staff. Promote information and use it to influence the attitude and behaviour of staff with regular short reminders.

Stakeholders

A stakeholder is anyone who has an interest in your school or MAT and is affected by its activity. There are many different stakeholders that we can engage with for different purposes, including income generation, marketing, support in dealing with issues, volunteering time and resources, and business sponsorship.

Personal and professional networks and groups:

- Pupils
- Parents and carers of pupils, grandparents, extended family and friends
- School governing bodies (including local governing body and Trust board members)
- School business leader groups
- Staff
- Senior leadership team
- Association of School and College Leaders (ASCL)
- National Association of Headteachers (NAHT)
- Institute of School Business Leaders (ISBL)
- National Governors Association (NGA)
- Alumni
- WomenED

Businesses and groups:

- Local businesses
- Larger companies with a CSR commitment
- Local business leaders and groups, *ie* Chamber of Commerce, WIRE
- Clubs and community groups
- Existing and potential school suppliers

Government organisations, groups and officials:

- Department for Education
- ESFA
- Charities Commission
- Local councillors
- Local authority

- Other agencies and public services *ie* health service, fire service, ambulance service and police
- Other education providers *ie* feeder schools/nurseries, future further education providers, work experience co-ordinators

Press and media platforms:

- Local TV regional news
- Education press publications
- Local newspapers, magazines and publications
- National press organisation
- Local radio station
- Social media, *ie* Twitter connections and chats, Facebook groups, pages and users, YouTube, LinkedIn, business links and groups
- Forums
- Bloggers

Charities and grant giving organisations:

These are the individuals, groups and organisations who are invested in what happens to your school or MAT and its pupils. They are a source of challenge and accountability, as well as being an essential resource. Consult them when necessary if you are considering changes that could potentially affect them. Utilise their support for marketing and income generation. Listen and engage with their criticisms and ideas, they are saying it because they care. Survey their views, they are your influencers and they can use this power positively or negatively, keep them informed and engaged.

Press releases

A press release generally has one of two main purposes, either responding to bad news, or celebrating good news.

You may be required to issue a proactive statement to pre-empt the release of a negative news story, this can help in that you are putting across the school's point of view first. Similarly you might need a reactive statement ready for when a news story does break or has already broken. There are some common threads to headlines or stories that you do not want, but may have to respond to:

- They are setting children up to feel like failures …
- Rise in unauthorised absences to blame for poor results …
- Action taken against drugs problem …
- Possible strike action over …
- School at breaking point over …
- The school had seen an alarming increase in …
- School rated 'inadequate' …

Then there are the less drastic but time-consuming issues which can be hard to resolve, for example you could be experiencing issues with parking and the local residents are unhappy. You may have addressed this by contacting the council and local police community support officers (PCSOs) to look at how signage, road markings and traffic management could improve the issue. The local residents are saying they are going to the press, so your school decides to pre-empt this by releasing their own statement, describing the action they have taken and the measures they have put in place to try to resolve the issue, thus showing the school in a positive light.

Positive press releases tend to be more proactive by nature as the school is usually aware of good news before the media, or they might be used when you are promoting an event, seeking funding, raising the profile of the school or aiming to maintain a positive brand image. It is good practice to raise awareness and publicity by publishing and promoting stories such as those concerning the opening a new playground, raising money for charity, good sports results, or academic achievement of an individual or group of students. These are the sorts of headlines we want:

- £10 million plan for local school …
- School choir wows the crowd at music event …
- Maths team seal their place in the next round …

- School achieves best results in their history ...
- Olympic hopes for youngster from local school ...
- School in top 10 ...
- School rated 'outstanding' ...

When writing your press release use verifiable facts and figures, along with good quality images (remember to check your photo consents before using images). In your first paragraph you need to get across why your news story matters. People are interested in reading about subjects that are innovative, different or new, and that are of public interest. Something really special may be of interest to local or national TV news, or even documentary makers, there have been many schools featured in programmes on education subjects.

You must have a great headline and use it in the subject line of the email to your PR contact database. Include relevant quotes in your press release, they should be an insightful reflection about the piece of news. Put your organisation's information separate to the body of the press release text.

Get a good 'hook' in to your first paragraph that grabs the readers' attention and conveys the essence of the story. Keep your press releases short, something like 300 to 400 words, in three to four short paragraphs, keeping everything clear and concise. Use sub-headings and bullet points to cover key information and avoid any education jargon that readers might not understand. Avoid grammatical and spelling errors and provide a link to further information, for example to your school web page.

The journalists looking at your press release will receive hundreds each day, and will have a couple of minutes, if that, to decide if your story is newsworthy enough for their publication. Make it as simple and easy as possible for them. If you are not successful the first time, do not give up, it may be that they have already filled their space and filed their content on that occasion, send out regular releases that are interesting and well written. Look in your local magazines and newspapers, what stories do they like to cover? What is interesting about them?

Be clear on what you are trying to achieve by issuing a story or press release. Are you looking to raise money? Attract business or volunteers? Raise the school profile?

Check that your press release passes the following tests:

- Is it new?
- Who will care about it?

- What is unusual about it?
- Will anyone outside of your school be interested?

Remember that press releases are as much for distribution on social media and blogs as they are for publication through traditional media formats, make the format suitable for all platforms or adjust it accordingly and have appropriate versions. If you are releasing something on social media, use influencers to expand the reach, tag them in the post and ask them to share it. If you are working with a company, charity or other organisation on a project, they may be able to get coverage in publications that they pay to advertise in.

Keep a list of publications and media outlets, there will be some that are useful for advertising school news and others such as industry publications and platforms which will be useful for sharing practice and experience from individual staff members or teams.

Top tip

Consent. Always, always check, double check and record photo consents for media usage.

Press release template

Design a press release template that you can issue to staff, they can fill in the basic details and send it back to you for refining. Consider which media outlets you are sending it to and format the style and language accordingly, *ie* local TV news, local newspapers and magazines, national press publications, education sector press, business management sector press, blogs, and local and regional radio stations.

Press Release Template

School name, address and logo
Website link and social media links
Release time, *ie* immediate or specific date

Date

Catchy headline
Subtitle

Top tips for writing a press release:

- Use a catchy headline
- Deliver the key message in the first sentence (15-20 words)
- Keep it succinct, with key information (300-400 words)
- Who, what, where, why and when
- Use facts and figures
- Add in quotes from key people
- Add photo and caption (if it shows staff or pupils, check consent)
- Use sub-headings and bullet points
- Finish with 'End'

END

About your organisation:

Summerise key information about your organisation that is relevant to the piece. Location, size, vision *etc.*

Contact details:

Name

Email

Phone number

Top tip

PR contacts. Build a database of press release contacts for local newspapers, radio, TV regional news, parish magazines *etc.*

Managing Time

If you work in school business management, then you know all about having to manage a heavy workload, conflicting deadlines, various responsibilities and high levels of accountability. I find that it is little things that make the difference can make life easier.

I work on the basis of small incremental improvements each day, which ultimately deliver effective and efficient services. Identify your time thieves and use time saving ideas. Set up good systems and processes and reduce duplication. Effective management of time is all in the planning.

The Covey quadrant

The Covey Quadrant (developed by Stephen Covey), is a time management matrix which can assist with deciding what to focus on. The key is to focus on what is important to You.

The four quadrants analyse the urgency and importance of tasks.

Quadrant 1
These tasks are urgent and important, this is where spend a lot of our time, dealing with the here and now, necessary and essential operational tasks such as emergencies, projects that are driven by deadlines, and preparation for scheduled events.

Quadrant 2
These tasks are important but not urgent, this is where we should be spending most of our time, but this tends not to happen because we are often in quadrants 1 and 3. This area is the most important because it is the time we spend planning, reflecting and creating. It is here that we exercise quality leadership, build and nurture relationships, accomplish personal and professional development, and spend time preventing negative issues from arising.

Quadrants 3 and 4 are the ones that we need to avoid, these are our time thieves.

Quadrant 3

These tasks are urgent but not important, and much like quadrant 1 this is where we can spend a lot of wasted time. This is a deceptive space, filled with things that are time-consuming but not important to us or our priorities; possibly some of the meetings we attend, interrupters and distractors and some communications. It is important to accept however that some of these things might be very important to those who bring them to us.

Quadrant 4

These are the tasks which are not urgent and not important. We should avoid these at all costs but unfortunately there are some which are hard to escape, such as junk emails, communications which are not relevant and time-wasting activities.

Try putting your tasks in to boxes and find out where you are spending most of your time.

1.	2.
3.	4.

Top tip

Focus on what is important to you. When I was writing this book, the timescale was tight and I had to fit it in around my other commitments. I kept a working copy with me and a notebook. When I had a spare few minutes, sat in the hairdressers or when my daughter was having a nap, I would use the time to make brief notes or self-edit.

View from an expert

Working across multiple schools – Louise Hatswell FISBL, director of finance/business manager, Saint Pius X Catholic High School, Rawmarsh St Joseph's Catholic Primary School and Our Lady and St Joseph's Catholic Primary School

Working across three schools (one secondary and two primaries) was a role that really appealed to me when I applied for it, and is one that I still find both interesting and challenging in equal measure. Working cross-phase after previously being in secondary was quite a transition. I have always felt that SBL colleagues in primaries do an absolutely sterling job; one-minute working on the budget, the next dealing with a cut knee or looking for a lost coat or PE kit. In smaller schools where the SBL is the only member of administrative and finance staff it must be an even more isolated role.

The biggest challenge I find in my role is capacity, there really is not enough time to do everything that is required of the role. I am based at the secondary school and my contract is split 60/20/20. Logistically this means that time is regularly spent travelling between schools, something I underestimate at times; a ten-minute journey really requires much longer as it is almost impossible to leave school without someone asking you something on the way to the car, and trying to find a parking space in or near the next school can be a time consuming challenge in itself. I have tried many ways of storing, filing and organising things and have found that it is easier to keep things separately, but to have a 'work in progress' file with current tasks and 'to do' lists for all schools that I can carry with me at all times. Remote access makes things much easier, but system and network restrictions and differences mean this is still far from ideal, although it is part of a longer-term plan. I also colour code my schools, and replicate this in my calendar and diary so I can see at a glance where I will be on any particular day.

An example of the challenges a role like this brings is when I recently received three budget allocations. Which to do first? Which second? How should I prioritise this? Another is preparing for and attending governing body meetings at three schools, which are often in the same week.

There are also benefits, it is possible to do some things with minimal adjustments or adaptations for use in all three schools, and I am streamlining more systems and procedures to work like this. There is a lot of potential for collaborative purchase across the schools which brings cost savings for all three, but the primaries in particular benefit from the economies of scale that working with the secondary brings.

Working off-site has proved very beneficial to me, as it allows me undisturbed time to work on complex issues, particularly budget monitoring and setting, and this is now part of my weekly working pattern.

Delegation

I read an interesting 2017 article by Val Andrew, ASCL Business Leadership Specialist, called 'Back to basic principles'. The piece was focused on the challenges facing the profession, time pressures and building capacity. In the article, Val referenced Jon Warner in his 2008 book 'Delegation'. In it Warner suggested that we should think about workload in terms of layers, rather like an onion has layers that can be peeled away, to get to the core.

At the centre are the tasks that you must do yourself, there are elements of our role, particularly the leadership elements, which it is not possible or appropriate to delegate to anyone else. For example, decision making on areas where we have the delegated authority to do so.

Then come the outer layers, and this is where there is potentially more flexibility, think about the following statements:

- Are there tasks that you are able and capable to do, but that other members of the team could assist with?
- Are there tasks that others can work on, that you could provide support and guidance with?
- Are there tasks which could be completed competently by others, either with or without some instruction, guidance or support?

Clarifying which of the three areas tasks fall in to can help with decision making concerning which tasks to delegate and which to focus your time on. Workload surveys have shown that SBMs work far more than their contracted hours, but there are only so many hours in the day, and we cannot do everything.

I have found that the better you get at your job, the more you will find is delegated to you. As one of the non-teaching and readily available members of the SLT, you will often become the go-to person for all sorts of things, and you should be very careful about what you take on yourself and what you accept the responsibility for dealing with. In the moment, when someone comes to you asking for help, it can be hard to say no or to re-direct them to someone else.

Effective delegation is a great skill to develop, ensuring that responsibility is fairly distributed between leaders and managers and that capacity is built in to our teams. That comes from the top down. An essential part of delegation is giving others the opportunity to develop their skills and broaden their knowledge and understanding; allowing them the creative space to find out things for themselves and develop their own methods, which may be an improvement on those in existence. As a business leader, I have always felt that it is important to be part of succession planning, both within the organisation that I work for and also the profession as a whole. I feel that we all have a duty to inspire and support the future generations of business leaders, to show them what we have learned from overcoming challenges and essentially how we have moved from surviving to thriving in our roles.

References

Andrew, V. (2017) 'Back to basic principles', *Leader* June 2017 (online). Available at www.leadermagazine.co.uk/articles/back_to_basic_principles/ (Accessed 16 Apr. 2018).

Warner, J. (2008) *The Delegation Pocketbook*. Arlesford: Management Pocketbooks.

View from an expert

Time management – Nickii Messer, school business management and leadership consultant; operational lead Anglia Ruskin University ILM SBM diploma programmes.

From my experience as an SBL and consultant I have found that the one thing there is never enough of is time.

I haven't met an SBL yet who hasn't found that work piles up, time runs out and they get dragged into a losing battle to get everything done. It can all appear completely overwhelming at times. Fighting with time is exhausting, stressful, and above all, utterly futile. The thing to understand is that you can't actually manage or control time itself. Time just ticks merrily on its way, with or without you. What you can control is yourself, your workload and the people you interact with.

Start by taking control of your workload before it takes control of you. There are many ways to do this, but the important thing is to find a method that suits you, then have the discipline to stick to it.

Take four files

Split your workload into four files – electronic or hard copies, whatever suits you best. Name these something like:

- Must do today
- Must do by tomorrow
- Must do this week

- Must do sometime

Split all your work into these four files. One hard and fast rule is that whatever goes in the 'Must do today' file must be non-negotiable, and must be completed. Continue the classification accordingly until everything is allocated to an appropriate file. This requires a bit of an investment in terms of time to get it started, but once it is done, you just need to readjust each evening before leaving your desk, and then add to the files accordingly every day.

In the morning, only open the 'Must do today' file and focus on getting those things done. Once these important, potentially urgent items are completed, you can move to the 'Must do tomorrow' file. Working in this way gives you control over your workload, and a wonderful sense of achievement when you progress from one file to the next – seemingly ahead of schedule. You are less likely to miss important deadlines too.

Diary

On the subject of deadlines, every SBL needs a diary to help control and allocate time. This is your plan of action, recording all project deadlines, as well as more obvious diary entries such as meetings and appointments. For more complex, time consuming projects set time aside in your diary to get started and continue progress ahead of deadlines, I call it slicing the elephant, cutting a large job down in to manageable parts in a sequential order. This can also give you useful prompts, reducing the risk of a last minute rush or a missed deadline. It is useful to insert dummy deadlines, so if something needs completing by Friday, enter a dummy deadline for Wednesday. When the inevitable happens and events overtake you and your good intentions, you will have allowed yourself plenty of time to take back control.

Prioritising

The effective SBL needs to allocate quality time to important strategic planning and development activities such as budgeting, staffing reviews, performance management and training, and designing systems and processes. The school's improvement or development planning template is a useful tool for this. Once these are listed, RAG rate them. The absolute imperatives, with high risk factors or deadlines are rated Red. It is Amber for those that are less urgent, less important, or not yet underway, and Green for the things you want to do, but are not essential, or can be left with minimal risk, or perhaps are already well underway or nearing completion. Allocate deadlines for each activity, remembering to put these in your diary, with prompts along the way.

Systems and processes

One of the biggest wastes of time in school offices is the lack of robust systems and processes. The 'we've always done it that way' mentality, leading to irrelevant, inefficient use of time. This situation requires an investment of time in order remedy it and create time saving systems and processes. It is imperative for the school that the SBL and support teams provide high-quality services in a business-like, time efficient way. Consider having specified opening times for administrative and finance teams to cut down on interruptions. What you actually create are closed times, where staff spend their time more effectively without constant interruptions that take them away from key tasks. Explain to stakeholders that this change aims to ensure a more efficient use of support time.

More top tips for better time-spending habits

- Focus on one thing at a time – our minds work better when focused on one thing at a time. Multitasking may seem a useful skill, but we are more productive when completing one task at a time.
- Avoid email overload – research proves that most of us waste a considerable amount of time each day just checking emails. Be disciplined and only check emails at set times. Let colleagues know you work like this.
- Divert or avoid interruptions – find ways to politely illustrate when you don't have time to be interrupted. Make appointments for colleagues to come back when you can allocate them quality time. Above all, don't let colleagues with poor organisational skills hijack your precious time.
- Delegate – either delegate whole tasks, or parts of tasks. Don't feel guilty about delegating responsibility to others in your team. This is how organisations grow and develop, and it allows the SBL to focus on responsibilities more suited to their strategic role.

- Know when to stop – recognise when something has been completed to a sufficiently high standard. You might prefer to spend more time perfecting it, but if that's not what you are paid to do, then don't do it.
- Eat Frogs – as Brian Tracy explains in his book 'Eat That Frog', if you have to eat a frog, get on and eat it. And if you have to eat more than one, tuck into the ugliest one first. This is a lesson in avoiding procrastination, a common time-wasting habit.

Finally

Put things into perspective. Your role is vital, but you are not a pilot or a surgeon, so if you run out of time, it is unlikely to be life or death. If it is a high-risk health and safety matter, put that at the very top of your list of things to do, in your 'Must do today' file. Everything else can wait. The bottom line is that the SBL role is all about supporting the wellbeing and life chances of the pupils. You have a duty to spend your time well.

Top tips

Eat the frogs first. Focus on one thing at a time, starting with the most urgent and important task. Avoid email overload by scheduling timeslots to look at emails. Do not use your email inbox as your to do list. Divert and avoid as many interruptions as possible. Delegate effectively. Know when to stop and when to rest, you are not a machine, to run effectively we need food, water and sleep.

Track traffic

Time is free but it's priceless. You can't own it. But you can use it. You can't keep it, but you can spend it. Once you've lost it you can never get it back.

Harvey MacKay (attrib.)

If you or one of your team are overwhelmed by requests or interruptions, then try doing a simple time and motion study. This is the observation of tasks over a period of time and can be a complex study where actions and timings of individual elements are recorded. It is often used when there are repetitive work processes or individual control elements making up a cycle. It is often used in the manufacturing industry, where they are looking at careful time management of individual tasks, and the optimal use of resources.

Try tracking for a day or a week why people are coming to see you and what they want or need.

Interrupters	Monday	Tuesday	Wednesday	Thursday	Friday
Order request	x	xx		xx	xxxx
Asking location of a member of SLT	xxxx	xxxx	xxxx	xxx	xxxx
Request for a mileage form					xxx
Staff asking about an absence request	x	x	x	x	x
Sales cold calls	xxxx	x	xx	x	xxx
Unscheduled meetings			x		

Tracking your interrupters will help you to identify patterns and causes. The tracking does not have to be onerous, for example start a simple tally chart. Once you know who and what the main interrupters are, then you can set to work on resolving the problem.

Colours and stamps

Have you ever noticed how clothes shops use colour coding to identify the different sizes? I saw a statistic that said our eyes identify colour coded files 40-45% faster than standard files. I find colour is easier and quicker to identify than words, although too many colours can complicate matters, so keep it simple.

You might want to colour code your files, for example keep all your H&S information in red files. If you work across a group of schools, have a different colour or stamper for each one. I use a different file colour for each of my schools and luckily each one has a different colour for their school brand, it is a useful visual. Segregate your in tray into types of work or in order of urgency, for example, having one for finance, one for HR or alternatively, one for must do today, must do tomorrow, must do this week, and so forth.

Block colour-coded sections in your diary for specific tasks such as meetings, interviews, lunch and do-not-disturb time.

Have simple stamps made for routine tasks, such as approving goods receipt notes and for coding and approving invoices. Have a school address stamp for use on official documents and use a date stamp post, so you know when items were first received.

Electronic notes and journals

Microsoft OneNote is a fantastic tool that has replaced my handbook. You can share notebooks with other staff, use sections and keep a task list.

We all have different ways of working. The way that works for me is not to try to populate my OneNote all in one go. I set aside small amounts of time, five or ten minutes where I can add a reference document or information. You can also use the print function to send information directly to your workbook. I have pages with documents, a 'to do' list, and a planner section where I add daily, weekly, monthly, termly and annual tasks, thus building up a business management electronic handbook.

Work experience

The next time that you are asked to have a work experience placement, a volunteer, a student placement or an apprentice, say 'Yes' immediately. They are a fantastic resource and an opportunity to have an extra person to assist with research and project work. As part of their placement you can set them some development tasks. I usually organise this as a pack of simple worksheets, which is useful as you can keep a copy on file and refer back to it if you are asked to be a referee.

Task 1

We are interested in identifying companies in the local area who would be interested in collaborating with our school in terms of providing sponsorship, volunteering or funding.

Please fill in the details below for companies that you think would be suitable.

Company name	What products do they make or what service or product do they sell?	Contact details (website address, contact name, telephone number and email address)	What do they offer?

Make sure that you take time to find out about any particular skills or interests they might have that could be useful. For instance, if they are very savvy when it comes to social media, ask them to look at how your school uses social media and whether they have any suggestions to improve it. What do they think? What are their ideas? Perhaps you are exploring business sponsorship opportunities. Ask the student to research which companies are in the local area and what projects they have recently funded.

Tips for being a good mentor, and giving the placement the best chance of being a success:

- Set up an outline plan of tasks and experiences with them, so you are both clear about what they will be doing during their placement.

- Allocate time to do mentoring, including one to one meetings and a meeting with their tutor.

- Make sure that they have a wide variety of work to do to broaden their experience.

- Ensure that they know how they fit in to the organisation and how their duties support the organisation in achieving its wider vision and objectives.

- Allow them time to do training, studies and research.

- Remember to cover essentials including an induction, H&S and safeguarding information.

- Allow them the space to make decisions and mistakes.

- Do not try to do everything for them.

- Be approachable and supportive, they should not be afraid to ask questions.

- Ensure that the wider team are supportive, giving help and guidance.

- Make them feel part of the team, include them in the tea rounds, invite them to school social events and tell them about things like dress down days that are happening. It is these little things that can make a big difference.

I have worked with some amazing apprentices, aspiring business managers and volunteers, who have added greatly to the development of the business management of the school. They were able to work independently, setting up new systems, drafting grant bids, researching business sponsorship opportunities, re-designing templates, and bringing their ideas forward with a fresh perspective.

Attendance reminder

What does good pupil attendance look like? For most schools it would be around 95% or above. Essentially this means not having more than ten days off in each school year.

Based on 190 days in the school year	Days of absence	Attendance percentage
Good attendance	Zero to ten days of absence	Between 95% and 100% attendance
Poor attendance	Between 20 to 30 days of absence	Between 90% and 85% attendance
Giving us cause for concern	Between 40 to 50 days of absence	Between 79% and 74% attendance

It is useful to remind parents and carers that there are 175 days when their child is not at school, and that these are ideal for non-urgent appointments. Ask them to plan in advance and help you to give their child the best opportunity to succeed.

Year planner

Most schools who are organised and plan well have a year planner that they issue to staff. Some schools also issue this to parents and carers and pupils or put key information on the school website or newsletter.

Many schools celebrate and take part in the same events each year such as religious or cultural festivals, world book day (very popular in primary schools and most parents' worst nightmare), sports days, parent and teacher meetings, celebration assemblies, performances, trips and visits, and examinations.

I have found it useful to create work planners with teams that assist with planning in advance for these events. I am a 'list person' who likes being organised and well prepared, and the use of work planners can help with managing the workload and prompting colleagues for things like letters or resource orders, and for planning staffing and cover arrangements. A lot of frustration is created when staff do not know what is going on and what is expected of them. We can alleviate some of that unnecessary stress and bad feeling through the use of good planning and communication.

There are many situations where it is useful; the caretaker ensuring that the field markings are done on time for sports day, organising the cleaning around evening events, the catering team linking themed food days with events, budget planning for resources, and ensuring that a senior leader is available and booked to introduce special events and present awards.

Month	Task
September	☐ Issue staff declaration form ☐ Issue consent form ☐ Remind staff about importance of consents ☐ Update and issue staff handbook and key policies ☐ Check through census information ready for autumn term submission ☐ Add key dates to newsletter and website ☐ Meet with clubs co-ordinator, issue letters and registers ☐ Check website compliance ☐ Check and book transport/accommodation/tickets for trips and visits ☐ Check policy schedule – issue reminder about policies that need to be reviewed ☐ Evacuation practice ☐ Lock down practice
October	☐ School photographer arrangements ☐ Parent/teacher meeting letters and booking arrangements – block book meeting rooms
November	☐ Send reminder to teachers about timeline for requesting orders for end of term activities ☐ Publicise fundraising events
December	☐ Issue letters/tickets to parents and carers for performances

Month	Task
January	☐ Check census information
	☐ Check and book transport/accommodation/ tickets for trips and visits. Send letters and supporting information
	☐ Add key dates to newsletter and website
February	☐ Order prizes and resources for World Book Day
March	☐ Preparation for pupil reports
	☐ Parent/teacher meeting letters and booking arrangements – block book meeting rooms
	☐ Evacuation practice
April	☐ Check and book transport/accommodation/ tickets for trips and visits
	☐ Place order for free items for new intake and prepare information packs
	☐ Add key dates to newsletter and website
	☐ Issue staff with a deadline for placing large resource orders for September
May	☐ Place order for leavers gifts, end of year awards and sports day medals/certificates
	☐ Evacuation practice
	☐ School photographer arrangements
June	☐ Issue reminder about year-end pupil reports
	☐ Promote online ordering for uniform
July	☐ Finalise and issue pupil reports
	☐ Inform parents and carers of new class information
	☐ Arrange file/information transfers

There are many other things that you can include on your planner such as open days, school milk requirements, assessments, data entry, invoicing, completing forms and returns, ordering, and meetings. It depends on what each individual or team is responsible for delivering so tailor it to their needs.

Life Savers

Is every one of your days full of happiness and wonderful life affirming achievements?

No, mine neither.

There are amazing days, usually involving making a difference to a young person, that make you feel that you are privileged and have the best job in the world. There are also days when you have been interrupted for the fiftieth time, you have a mountain of work, it all feels overwhelming and that you must be insane to want to work in schools.

Then there are all those other days that fly by while you tackle every task and responsibility from drafting the five-year budget plan to ensuring that all the medals and certificates are ready for sports day and then doing a lunchtime playground duty.

Here are some ideas to get you through the tough days, the exhausting days, even the darkest days.

View from an expert

Collaboration – Nickii Messer, school business management and leadership consultant; operational Lead Anglia Ruskin University ILM SBM diploma programmes.

Throughout the years I have worked with school business managers and leaders, one of the most rewarding aspects of group training activities has been the proactive and empathetic networking that results from them.

Networking is something that SBLs do really well and there are many opportunities to join groups of like-minded colleagues, both physically at meetings and conferences, or virtually through social media, (especially Twitter and LinkedIn).

Ironically, surrounded by people as the SBL will be in their school, the role can still be a very lonely one. It is unlikely that there will be anyone else in the school with a similar role, and therefore no-one else who really understands the challenges, stresses and the pressure of the 'crunch' times.

While networking with other SBLs is an important element of professional development – and sanity – working collaboratively goes beyond this type of group activity. In particular, collaborative working within the school is essential for the SBL.

One of the most important collaborative relationships for the SBL will be with the headteacher or principal. Both need to be able to forge positive and intrinsic links between teaching and learning and the business of the school. For collaboration to work effectively each party must be able to understand the other, and both must work within a context of trust, shared values and goals. As with any relationship, this requires commitment to one another as well as to the relationship itself. With so many demands on the time of both parties, the SBL will need to be proactive in ensuring that regular meetings happen. Get these set into the diary and draw up a standard agenda to work from. This investment of time will pay dividends for the SBL and headteacher alike, and ultimately the school and the children.

Similarly, to be able to contribute fully to the SLT it is important to work collaboratively, sharing duties, contributing to agendas, and attending all aspects of every meeting. Credibility can be an issue, so act, walk and talk like a leader and read as much as possible about the world of education to keep informed and up to date. One of the things that I found most helpful when I was an SBL was to attend conferences and briefing events for headteachers. These not only helped me understand and keep myself current within the world of strategic school leadership but enabled me to network and learn from some really inspiring senior colleagues.

Too many schools still feel they have a 'them and us' culture, dividing teachers and support staff. In such a situation the SBL has an opportunity to effect positive change. Working collaboratively with all parties can do so much good in ensuring a better understanding of each other's perspective. Too often support staff in particular decry the fact that teachers fail to understand them, but then do nothing to promote better understanding. The important first step when faced with this issue is to analyse what is happening and why. What are the root causes? Then, don't accept the status quo, challenge and commit to improving it, especially when it is detrimental to the overall health of the organisation. Some of my own tried and tested methods for the SBL to reduce misunderstandings and promote cohesion:

- Encouraging all support staff to attend staff meetings and briefings. Just because they might not be invited doesn't mean they can't go.
- Use staff induction and INSET training sessions to explain the various functions of the business management and support staff roles.
- Talk with teachers and department heads to better understand their perspective. Asking to visit and spend time in the classroom, as well as talking to staff in the staff room, are both good ways to do this.
- Hold meetings and INSET sessions for support staff, and include news about teaching and learning, and explain what is happening in the classrooms.
- Get to know all of your colleagues, whatever their role, and give them every opportunity to get to know you too, both personally and professionally.

One of the most important responsibilities for the SBL is to ensure that all resources are used to their optimum efficiency, with the very highest quality of support service delivered at all times. Working collaboratively with key stakeholders will ensure that all parties understand how best to make this happen and will create a common cause to make sure that it does.

How to survive

I remained strong. The hills phase had taught me that I didn't need to be faster, tougher or smarter than anyone else. I just had to rely on my own mental and physical strengths to get through, rather than measuring myself against the successes and failures of those around me.

Colin Machlachlan

The main way to survive and be successful in our roles is to focus on being a strategic leader, but we all know that schools do not work like this all the time. There is no direct path to success but there are small wins each day that add up to big improvements. There are always going to be times when we will need to deal with all sorts of issues that are inside and outside of our remit.

One thing that I have found is that it can be easy to be caught in the 'busyness trap' and others can often cause that. It can also be hard when you start in a new organisation and no one has the time, or worse the inclination, to help you in learning what you need to know. Everyone benefits in the long term if we spend time showing colleagues how things work.

For example, it is a Friday afternoon and the head of English comes rushing in to your office. They are having a nightmare, a class is due to start reading a new book next week and they are five copies short. It is someone's fault and it has to be sorted. They need the other five books for Monday, all of their planning has been tailored around reading the first chapter of the book. The head of English wants to how you are going to sort it out.

Is it important and vital to you? No.

Is it important and vital to them? Yes.

How would you deal with this situation?

Would you get online straight away and order an express delivery? This maybe the quickest way to sort the problem. Nevertheless, if your budget is tight, can you afford to place the order? Perhaps you would you analyse the situation and collect information; How many children are in the class? How many books did we order? Have they all arrived? If not, do we have an expected delivery time for the outstanding portion of the order? It could be that the order was only placed last week and that you have received a part delivery. Have other possibilities been explored, such as sending out a message to all staff, and asking if anyone has a copy that they could donate/loan.

I am not belittling teachers here or saying that it is their fault. We all know the colleagues we work with who are super organised and those who leave everything to the last minute. Along with those who are respectful and understand that you have lots to do and those who are the exact opposite.

What I am highlighting is that it is easy to be drawn in and influenced by the other person's urgency without really thinking the situation through. In these situations I advise people to sit down and explain to me what has happened, and I assure them that we will find a way to resolve the issue.

Be good at building and developing effective relationships and efficient teams, getting this right will pay off in the long term. Focus on roles not people, getting the staffing structure right that will ensure that you will provide the best business management function possible.

Successful people:

- continuously learn – constantly challenge yourself.
- create trust, give compliments and say thank you – inspire people to be as passionate about business management as you are.
- embrace change – progress without change is impossible.
- forgive others – being positive in a negative situation is not naïve, it is leadership
- discuss ideas – take every opportunity to communicate and develop ideas.
- accept responsibility – always.
- be goal orientated – a goal should scare you a little bit but excite you a lot. Make it happen.

Plan time to work away from school

You have to decide what your highest priorities are and have the courage – pleasantly, smilingly, non-apologetically, to say 'no' to other things, and the way you do that is by having a bigger 'yes' burning inside.

Stephen Covey

Time to plan and reflect, or to work undisturbed on an important piece of work or project, will improve your productivity and help you to manage your work-life balance.

It is likely that there is only you in your school who does what you do. Who else is going to prepare the budget plan and come up with creative ideas for making it balance, or prepare a report for the board on the long term financial plan? You are also likely to be responsible for the operational and/or strategic delivery of many different areas. This makes your time precious, because there will not be someone else picking up those tasks. You should put great value on your time and what you do with it. Without the constant interruptions you will get much more done. I would recommend that you plan to work away from school at least once each half-term, it is important that senior leaders demonstrate a good work-life balance.

Here are some tips for making your time away from the office most productive:

- Put an out of office message on your emails and don't access them.
- Set a schedule which includes breaks.
- Do not multi-task, stick to the specific tasks and focus on what matters.

I often say the words 'single focus' to myself, it reminds me to focus on getting one thing done properly at a time.

Learning library

Read, reflect, learn, repeat

I read to learn from the experiences of others who have taken a different path to me, and you can create your own learning library. Do not throw away all those CPD workshop notes or magazines, as you progress through your career, they can come in useful and you never know what direction the next opportunity will take you.

Resource bank

You could set up your own business management learning library, a bank of resources for you and your team to utilise for development. It is also useful if you are mentoring a member of staff who is undertaking a course or if you decide to do a Masters or PhD. I have set up a bank of files with sections for each of the ISBL Professional Standards. I keep and file workshop notes, articles, research papers, templates and reports that I find interesting.

Books, books, books

I am creating my own leadership learning library of books, investing in publications that other business management professionals have recommended, and I try to read one each month.

Book recommendations:

- 'High Challenge, Low Threat' Mary Myatt
- 'Leadership Matters' Andy Buck
- 'Educating Drew' Drew Povey
- 'Making the Leap' Dr Jill Berry
- 'Our Iceberg is Melting' John Kotter and Holgar Rathgeber
- 'Don't Change the Lightbulbs' Rachel Jones
- 'The Virgin Banker' Jayne-Anne Gadhia
- 'Lean In' Sheryl Sandberg
- 'Thrive' Arianna Huffington

Whole school approach

Some schools make it part of the school improvement and development plan to encourage and expect staff to read as part of their professional development. Here are some of the approaches they take:

- Reading the same article or blog post for a staff meeting discussion.
- A termly or monthly book club.
- Purchasing a book for every member of staff at the beginning of the year.
- Building a staff library of books and encouraging staff to request books that they would like to add to the library.
- Setting challenge sheets or gap tasks.
- Putting together a selection of reading materials on different subjects which are relevant to school development areas.

Top tip

Audio books and podcasts are brilliant for long commutes.

View from an expert

How to survive as a school business manager – Peter Neale MSc FISBL, school business leader

It can sometimes feel lonely as a school business manager. In many schools the SBM occupies a unique position: neither a teacher nor truly a member of support staff but somewhere undefined and in-between.

Often the SBM is the only person with knowledge, experience and responsibility in specific areas – particularly finance in these austere times – and will be acutely aware that, when faced with a progressively challenging set of circumstances, the school community increasingly relies upon them to act in a decisive, professional and effective manner.

Several years ago, feeling somewhat isolated and overwhelmed, I co-founded a local school business managers' association with a few other SBMs who, I was surprised to find, were all feeling just as vulnerable as me. We met each half term at one another's schools and, within a short period, our small group had grown to welcome members representing all types of educational establishments located throughout the local authority area. There was a great deal of mutuality between us, and we soon found that we could share our best methods of overcoming commonly faced obstacles and could offer invaluable advice to one another about how best to avoid mistakes, as well as recommending suppliers offering best value. Some while later the group affiliated to the National Association of School Business Management (NASBM), opening up wider networking opportunities.

Over the years, I have discovered a variety of ways of coping with the stresses and pressures of everyday SBM life. None of them is difficult, and most are pretty obvious. So, if you're feeling lonely and frustrated, rather than kicking the cat when you get home in the evening or drowning your sorrows in a vat of wine, you may instead wish to take some of these steps:

Don't keep it to yourself

- Reduce stress levels by discussing problems with people in a similar situation.
- Speak regularly with your headteacher, governors and colleagues.
- Visit other SBMs at their schools, especially within your Trust or Federation if you have one.
- See how other people tackle issues and listen to their concerns, no doubt you will uncover a great deal of common ground.

Network with others

- Join a local SBM Group.
- Share best practice and procure together.

- If there isn't a local group, either start one with your neighbouring SBMs, Trust or Federation, or join an SBM association further afield.
- Join ISBL
- Join a professional association such as ASCL or NAHT.
- Join the Financial Directors' Forum (FDF).
- Correspond with like-minded SBMs on Twitter or LinkedIn.

Keep yourself informed

The more you understand, the better prepared and more confident you will be in overcoming issues. Try subscribing to these newsletters, (there are many more):

- ESFA e-bulletin.
- GOV.UK Weekly Digest Bulletin.
- SSAT Sunday Supplement.
- School Financial Success.
- Independent Schools Council Daily News Summary.

Take a course

Some of the best people you will ever meet can be found on SBM training courses:

- ILM Level 4, 5 and 6 qualifications (formerly CSBM, DSBM and ADSBM), CIPFA financial reporting qualifications

Concentrate on developing your emotional intelligence

Learn how:

- to persist in the face of frustrations.
- to control impulse and delay gratification.
- to regulate one's moods and keep distress from swamping your ability to think.
- to empathise and to hope

(Goleman, 1996)

Poor time management can result in bad decision-making and underperformance, leading to a downward spiral of increased pressure and stress.

Effective time management, however, is based on quality rather than quantity; doing important things well rather than ticking off every task on an impressively long list. Learning how to manage your time will help prevent wasted energy and enable you to focus on the most important things. With better control of your time, I promise that you will become more relaxed and less anxious.

Here are a few ideas to help reduce a school business manager's often disproportionately long working week:

- Don't keep a 'To Do' list in your head but put it on paper or, better still, your computer.
- A well-planned system ensures smooth workflow and will keep everything organised.
- For example, I rely heavily on the 'Tasks' and 'Calendar' functions of Microsoft Outlook.
- Clear your desk – stacks of paper will distract your focus
- Set aside time to plan your day, at the end of each day – whenever I can, I map out the next day's tasks so that I can go home without having to worry too much and can sleep more soundly.
- Make good use of your calendar – do not over-schedule yourself, wherever possible leave gaps between meetings to allow time to reflect and also catch up, and allow time for interruptions.
- Share your schedule with others – reception staff can act as effective gatekeepers, keeping away unwanted phone calls and other distractions.
- Work from home on occasion – if at all possible negotiate with your school to allow you to work from home on the most important tasks.
- Never buy from cold callers – while I will take unsolicited calls from time to time, I make a point of never buying from them and will politely and firmly discourage them from calling back.
- Use email rather than phone:
  o When someone telephones me I have to stop what I'm doing and work to their agenda. With an email, within reason, I can choose when to answer.
  o An email provides an audit trail – readily available evidence of who said what, and when.

- Take your time to react (unless it's a fire alarm) – be patient and accept that you can't respond to everything instantly.
- Be decisive:
  - o Don't waste time prevaricating, develop the ability to make effective, clear decisions.
  - o Say 'no' more often and learn how to decline unnecessary opportunities.
- Focus – while there will always be something else competing for your attention, unless you are an accomplished multi-tasker try to shut everything out and concentrate on the task at hand.
- Make time for others (but not too much):
  - o Be there for colleagues and encourage them but make it clear when you have plenty to get on with.
  - o Be assertive (not aggressive) with those who try to drain your time and energy.
  - o Value your time and other people will surely do the same.
- Be ruthless with meetings – always try to set an agenda and a finishing time, there are countless examples of weakly-chaired governors' meetings going on for hours.
- Start early – arriving early provides a priceless uninterrupted run up to the day. I began this practice many years ago after 17 windows were smashed along the front of my school. Arriving early gives you time to think and react before everyone arrives.
- Delegate:
  - o Don't be too proud to ask for help.
  - o If you do not think there is anyone who would complete a task to your high standards, why not train them how to do it? It'll take a little longer at the outset but will empower them and hopefully give them confidence to help more in the future.
- Use commuting time to reflect or unwind – when I play my favourite music in the car I can feel the day's anxieties melt away.

My late father had a positive outlook on life and whenever matters seem overwhelming, I try to keep his advice in mind. 'Never mind, son,' he used to say, 'try to keep things in perspective: always remember that we're warm, we know where our next meal is coming from, and nobody is trying to shoot at us.'

References

Goleman, D. (1996) *Emotional Intelligence: Why It Can Matter More Than IQ.* London: Bloomsbury.

Top tips

Manage time, do not let it manage you. Network and collaborate with other SBMs. Make time to get out of school. Accept that you will not be able to do everything, but you can do what matters the most and will have the most impact. Know that you are not alone.

Blogging

Blogs are widely used by teachers and other education professionals from all over the world. They are often used to demonstrate and share expertise, knowledge, examples of good practice and views on current topics of interest.

Business managers have often said to me that they are concerned about blogging or posting on social media because of confidentiality, and of course, it is important that you are not sharing information that you should not be. This does not preclude you from writing with your views and ideas on your areas of interest and expertise. I have used writing for a while now as a way sharing my expertise and knowledge, but also as part of my wellbeing. When I am having a tough day or week, I will write things down and often the problems seem much smaller.

Do not feel overwhelmed and think that you need to write a huge amount, some of the best posts are short and to the point, aim for about five hundred words. Writing can develop in to something that is powerful and influential and can provide a useful and entertaining resource for school business professionals. Starting a blog can also lead to other opportunities, for instance @WorkingSBM2017 is also a conference speaker and writes for an industry magazine.

Here are some ideas to help you decide what to write about and get you started:

- Email a business manager or senior leader colleague that you admire, ask them three questions and use the answers to form a post.
- Write an account of your experience attending an event or conference. What were the highlights? Who did you meet? What did you talk about?

- Brainstorm ideas for a series of posts on your main area of expertise. Start with a bullet point outline. For example, if you focused on a series about budgeting it could be:

  o Post 1 – outlining the annual processes, key dates, why budgeting is important, what the series will cover.

  o Post 2 – budget setting, using zero based or previous outturn, how to decide where you make savings or expect to see increases, how to budget for delegated and self-generated income.

  o Post 3 – how and when to present this information to key stakeholders, how to make it understandable.

  o Post 4 – benchmarking, why it is useful, how to do it, when to do it.

  o Post 5 – budget monitoring, how and when to do it.

Top tip

Finding a topic to blog about; in order to generate ideas for my own writing I go through recent articles and write down headlines that I find interesting, this can often spark an idea. Also look out for blog challenges, often shared on social media.

View from an expert

Why do I blog? – @WorkingSBM2017, School Business Leader

You don't write because you want to say something, you write because you have something to say.

F. Scott Fitzgerald

At the beginning of last year, I suddenly found that I had a lot to say. Education funding had reached a critical point, changes in the structure of my school had doubled my workload and I could see my colleagues were in a downward spiral, dispirited and pessimistic. I knew I was becoming stressed and I needed to do something to help myself. With no clear idea of what I was doing or why, I started a new year blog to release some of the tension and slot my concerns into some semblance of order in my own head.

Surprisingly I found it to be immensely enjoyable and productive, my stress levels reduced and with my own head clearing, I began to see ways to move forward and support my colleagues during the challenges we faced.

When I also started promoting my blog on social media I discovered that there were many SBLs around the country in similar situations and they valued a voice just telling them 'you're not alone'.

I don't want to give the impression that readership of my blog is significant because, although growing, it is still small. I know I write for a very niche sector of professionals, most of whom are still very wary of the compatibility of engaging in social media and working in a school, so I regularly remind myself of the reasons that I write.

For my own wellbeing

Writing enables me to express my frustrations and worries, as well as my excitement and optimism for the future of education in this country. I try not to limit my subject matter and I often just write about how I'm feeling. Sometimes it is work specific and sometimes it is not, work-life balance is important in blogging too!

To feel connected to other SBLs

Through my followers and conversations on social media I feel connected to other SBLs, we are all going through the same challenges and they are honest with their feedback which encourages me to learn, grow and continue writing.

Collaboration

I've discovered that the SBL's capacity to collaborate, share good practice and be professionally generous, is enormous. The ideas that swirl around a topic of conversation on social media has led to many positive developments in my work. My confidence has grown, my ability to self-reflect has increased and, after fifteen years as an SBL, I really feel there is a community out there that has my back.

To give something back

I personally get so much from my writing that I'm keen to give something back with articles and blogs that are supportive, informative and enjoyable to read. Being an SBL might be challenging but it is also a lot of fun and I try to communicate how much I love my job in my writing, an SBL always has an eye on succession planning!

Blogging is not for everyone, whether it is writing themselves or reading others' blogs, it takes up time and requires thought and planning (usually after you have spent the day thinking and planning at work). You have to be relatively consistent in output to maintain your readership and it can divert attention away from what you should be doing. However, it can also be an excellent stress reduction tool and a good way to meet other SBLs, share good practice, learn, collaborate, and cultivate an outward facing attitude to work and education.

Of course, the challenges in my work haven't gone away, education funding is still shockingly insufficient, my workload continues to grow and my colleagues still need my support, but I am now able to shout about it from my blog. Talking to other SBLs, resolving issues and working together to develop the profession, all helps me to improve my own performance and contribution at work, and I enjoy the process of writing. Now I'm in a much better place, I'm more productive, I'm more able to support my colleagues, I'm sleeping at night, I've made so many friends at home and abroad, and I'm getting much more out of my role as a school business leader.

How to deal with imposter syndrome

Remember, no one can make you feel inferior without your consent.

Eleanor Roosevelt (attrib.)

I respect hierarchy and those who hold senior or significant roles, this was something I learned at school, where we were taught to respect adults and those in authority. I am embarrassed to admit this, but I often get a bit star struck when I meet people who I follow on social media.

I have had that feeling sat around a table with other education leaders, debating issues, and thinking; How did I get here? What can I possibly add to a conversation that includes these people, who I respect and admire? Or standing up to do a presentation to a room of school business leaders and asking myself what I could possibly have to tell these people that they do not already know.

My husband is always good at helping me in these situations, when my confidence is not as strong as it should be, and he will remind me that whatever role someone performs, they are still just a person. Value what you know, you would not have been invited to an event if you did not have something add.

I was asked to step in to speak about 'Better Buying' at the ASCL Business Leaders Conference when the Department for Education representative booked to do the session, had to withdraw at last minute. During the session, there was a man writing notes, lots of them. He asked some questions too, which I was able to help with. Chatting with him after the session finished it transpired that he had been in post a matter of weeks, this was his first school business leader event, and he wanted to learn as much as could to take back to his new school.

I also had a conversation with the brilliant Nickii Messer about facilitating workshops, and how to effectively do an interactive task-based workshop, rather than a formal presentation. She gave me a great piece of advice, which was that not everyone knows what you know, and if they have chosen to come to your session, it is because they are interested in the topic. It was a good reminder that there are people with varying levels of experience, knowledge and skill.

I am far from knowing everything about education, business management and leadership. I will never know everything. If I do not know the answer to a question, I will say so and look it up later, and more importantly I am not afraid of saying 'I am sorry if this is silly question, but can you explain that to me'.

Public speaking

I've learned that people will forget what you said, people will forget what you did, but people will never forget how you made them feel.

Maya Angelou

Public speaking is the single most difficult challenge that I have personally faced. I used to be terrified and I know many colleagues who have faced the same fear.

I overcame it by working with supportive colleagues who gave me advice and the confidence to keep trying and to eventually learn not to overcome but to manage my fear, especially the outward symptoms. I still get nervous now, but in a healthy way. I would never want to become somebody who thought they knew it all. Personally, I find it harder to speak in front of a group of people I know, than an audience of strangers.

Seek out places to practice your speaking, try different sized spaces and project your voice. Accept that there are going to be unknowns, when the ICT breaks down, the fire alarm goes off or someone asks a question to which you do not know the answer. Start small and build your way up. I would often practice to an empty room so that I could try different voice levels and standing in different places. You do not need to be funny; people are not looking for a comedy performance.

Practice breathing and pace. A colleague once told me that it was important as a leader to always be calm and commented that I would often be in rush when speaking or walking. Think of a swan on a lake, gliding beautifully across the water, while frantically paddling underneath to move from one point to the next. If I find myself rushing through a speech or almost running to my next meeting, I start singing 'Moon River' in my head.

Look at the people in the audience and keep moving around their faces. Do not stand at the front looking down and read from a piece of paper. I have notes with me to refer to, but I try not to be over reliant on them. Use anecdotes from your own experiences. This can often be a good way to start a presentation. If it is an experience that you have shared before, you will be confident of the details and it helps to set the stage for what you will be delivering in the session.

Sometimes it can be hard to decide how to start your presentation, but you do have some options.

Start with a story:

> *In my past life as a soccer coach once you win a National Championship everyone wants to come play for you.*

> Dr Ivan Joseph

> *When I was nine years old I went to summer camp for the first time and my mother packed me a suitcase full of books.*

> Susan Cain

Quote another inspiring leader:

> *Martin Luther King had a dream, we all know the dream that Martin Luther King had, he had a dream about social integration, as opposed to social separation.*

> Hannah Wilson

Ask the audience to do something:

> *Ok, I need a favour, all the girls between the age of 17 and 24 stand up.*

> Courtney Ferrell

So, for any of us in this room today let's start by admitting we are lucky. We don't live in the world our mothers, our grandmothers lived in, where career choices for women were so limited.

Sheryl Sandberg

Have something strong and positive to finish with, for example provide reassurance, offer options, or challenge the audience by asking them to do something after the session. You can practise your public speaking skills in the following ways:

- Do a school assembly.
- Present at a staff meeting.
- Deliver a workshop at an SBL event.

Top tip

Always keep a glass of water to hand, it helps in case you start to get a dry throat and it is something to focus on if there is a suitable pause.

Next steps

In order to get better at something feedback is important. With this in mind, I made a home video of myself presenting on the topic of benchmarking. I uploaded it to YouTube and asked trusted peers for feedback. Although this experience was outside of my comfort zone, I knew that I needed honest feedback in order to improve my practice. It was a useful exercise and I gained much more than I expected. I was given feedback and advice on how I could structure the presentation differently, by using an outline, summarising and repeating key points to reinforce understanding, not try to cover too much in one go, and add in evidence-based facts and figures.

Collaboration

Without trust we don't truly collaborate, we merely co-ordinate or, at best, co-operate. It is trust that transforms a group of people in to a team.

Stephen Covey

Peer support

Peer support can come in different forms, often the most valuable part of attending conferences can be the informal chats that you have with other delegates. Peers can also be a great source of feedback, and all good leaders make time for gaining feedback.

When we network we can share messages and information about operational changes, strategic plans, and improvements, and we can share best practice that allows us to stay relevant and up to date. These discussions need to continue because our work and practice is continually evolving to meet the needs of a changing educational landscape.

There are many formal and informal ways of working together:

- Join a school business leaders' group.
- Attend CPD events.
- Attend conferences.
- Attend panel debates and special interest groups, facilitated by government or professional organisations.
- Consultations and questionnaires.
- Undertake a professional qualification in school business management or leadership.
- Social media – check your organisation's policy and consider carefully whether you want to have your profile as private or public.
- Link with another school.
- Collaborate online.
- Share your good practice.
- Collaborative purchasing.
- Support, mentoring and coaching.
- Networking.
- Set up or join a peer support group.

View from an expert

An SBM's lifesaver – Maggie Duncan FISBL, school business manager and LASBM member

Your local SBM groups are a true lifesaver for any SBM, finance director, COO or office manager. It may be small group of local primary or secondary schools, or one of the many county groups that are now being set up, ISBL can put you in touch with your local groups.

I belong to LASBM (Lancashire Association of School Business Managers). I access this group via their online forum and three annual conferences. I have asked many 'stupid' questions over the years and been given an array of responses from a vast pool of knowledge. I can guarantee that whatever you are experiencing is also being experienced by, or has been experienced by another person in the group. These groups are non-judgemental and supportive and are often the first port of call for sharing best practice or to find out about the latest legislation or guidelines. We may all share similar job titles but that does not mean that we are all the same personality, and a group setting allows all of these personalities to thrive. The conferences also allow much-needed time to reflect on your own decisions and setting, registration or membership is usually free or for a nominal amount. As part of the county groups you also have access to keynote speakers and group purchasing discounts.

I am also a member of ISBL (Institute of School Business Leaders) and often go to their free regional events. If you really want to immerse yourself in an information-dense environment, their national conference is the place to go. I have taken my headteacher for the last two years.

Whole school collaboration

A primary school in Leeds won a national collaboration award recently for reportedly engaging with over a thousand volunteers from within the local community to support teaching and learning. Their activities included reading volunteers, solicitors supporting maths, the local bank supporting the teaching of mental arithmetic, enterprise mentors teaching business fundamentals and pupils going out to visit companies to raise aspirations.

I have worked in an area of high deprivation and I know that it is essential to inspire children and show them that a bright future is possible, and to foster their interest in areas they aspire to work in. We can be part of breaking the cycle of a child becoming a third or fourth non-working generation in a family.

Collaboration – Dawn Boyes MA FISBL, head of finance business partnering, United Learning

The discussion of collaboration verses competition has been one which has been raging since I began in the profession in the 1990s. During this time, we have seen soft and hard federations, clustering, academisation and MATs all developing. There is competition for exam results fuelled by the ever-increasing number of published statistics about school performance. There is competition for pupils to enrol in your school fuelled by the per pupil funding. And at the same time, we are under pressure to ensure cost efficiency and value for money.

One thing is for certain; with the tightening of funding, collaboration to increase efficiency in schools is becoming more important again. There are numerous forms of collaboration which can include educational collaboration but for the school business leader the key area which I would like to concentrate on is efficiency through back office services collaboration.

In a MAT you may see central services which cover some of this role, in effect they are small scale local authorities, but that does not mean that you have to be in a set structure to make efficiency savings.

Communication

Communication is key, when you collaborate it is important to clearly define who is responsible for what, where and when. If done well there are clear communication channels and everyone knows what is expected regarding the goals and outcomes. When done badly it can lead to resentment, misunderstanding, a blame culture and the onus being on one person. There needs to be a clear division of roles and responsibilities, as well as clear expectations. In order to do this, you have to be able to pull the key players together on a regular basis to ensure that goals and targets are being met and to respond to any changes.

It is also important to be realistic and by measuring outcomes you will know what works and what doesn't. There is no use expending huge effort for very little reward unless it also brings other benefits to your organisations.

Consistency

In order for collaboration to work, you need buy in from everyone, from the senior leadership, those making purchasing decisions, and those actually placing the orders in each school. There is little point in negotiating a group deal and setting a long term price only for one school to say they are taking a better offer from an online provider. That would not only jeopardise the price for others, but it is also a waste of time and effort all round.

Vision

When setting up any form of collaboration, it is important to start with the vision – why are we doing this and what do we want to achieve? This sets the foundations and if these are firm it will aid communication and you are more likely to get consistency and buy in. Collaboration can often come with the fear that it might signal the start of a takeover.

In the past, I have used the analogy of the weekly shop to demonstrate some ideas behind my attitude to purchasing. I can buy a medium sized chicken for £5, that is just enough for my family's Sunday dinner. But if I buy a large chicken for £6, I can make two more meals for later in the week. If I did not have a family, why should I buy an individual portion of chicken breast for £3.50 when I could buy a large chicken for £6 and divide it in to portions for a cost of £1.50 each? If we do that with our weekly shopping, why don't we do it with education funding?

So why don't we do it?

Well, sometimes the answer will be fear, and it comes back to competition versus collaboration. In this case the key is vision. If our shared vision is to ensure we have the best resources for all students in the education system and to give all students every opportunity to reach their goals, then the premise behind collaboration is much clearer.

In other cases, it may be a lack of knowledge or enthusiasm which holds people back. If you are not in an established school grouping the starting point could be your regional school business manager network. Here

217

like-minded people are grappling with the same issues. Start with the basics and work up. Identify what you all use, such as regional newspaper advertising, or paper call off, and decide what you want to achieve. Set clear roles, responsibilities and expectations – get the headteachers and governors to buy in to your vision.

These are starting points which can lead to efficiency savings and can slowly lead to further collaboration as systems and processes become embedded. School funding is not a bottomless pit. We owe it to our students to look at systems that are cost effective and ensure the best resources are available for all. In competition there are winners and losers, in collaboration we all work together towards being on the winning team.

Setting up a peer support group

Setting up your own local peer support group can be useful to you and your school. School business leader groups are brilliant for CPD and networking, but large groups do not suit everyone, and there often is not the time to get in to detailed discussions about specific topics. A smaller local group provides an opportunity to focus on relevant issues with others who are in a similar setting and location, and you can set the agenda. Teachers moderate what they do, and we as school business professionals should do the same.

To set up your own peer support group, start by inviting one or two like-minded professionals to meet with you. Aim to meet once each half-term, setting aside one or two hours. At the first meeting decide on the topics and areas that you want to cover and what the outline for the meetings will be. It is useful to set up an agenda and take minutes as evidence of the impact that this activity is having.

There is so much scope for what you can cover in these meetings:

- Sharing good practice and procedures.
- Supporting and encouraging one another.
- Comparing costs and services to see where you can improve value for money.
- Working together on projects and sharing the workload utilising each individual's skills.

Be clear about confidentiality and ensure that the information is not shared outside the group without permission. Keep staff and pupil information and data anonymous. For the group to work well, it is vital that there is trust between you.

Next steps

When you are ready, and when the group is established, invite others to join and grow the group. Inviting others will change the dynamic of the group, but it will also bring fresh perspectives, experience and ideas.

How to get networking right

Start with considering what you want to get from networking. Do you want to meet people who are doing a similar role? Do you want to meet someone who has a particular area of knowledge or expertise? Do you want to expand your reach in your local area? Do you want to meet potential employers?

When I am going to an event on my own, I will look online to see who else is going and have a couple of people in mind to introduce myself to. Business management conferences and CPD events provide a great opportunity to meet and network with peers.

However, what about potential next employers? I attended a WomenEd event that gave me some great advice on how to master this; you have to fill their space. Social media is one way, but not all headteachers, CEOs and board members have the time or inclination to use it regularly. Think about the type of event you can attend where there are opportunities to highlight your talents or meet these people, if you go to a conference for governors and SLT members, then that's who you will be talking with. Be confident in your skills, knowledge and value, and try not to be intimidated by titles.

Attend different types of events such as regional and national conferences, specific training, breakfast meetings, roundtable and panel debates, and social media chats, they will all have something to offer you. At a careers themed CPD event I went to there was a workshop where you were given feedback on your CV, covering letter, application form or personal statement. I took along a copy of the last application form that I had submitted, and although I was not looking for another job it was a great opportunity to learn.

Hosting events

I have been to many conferences and CPD events and I have made some observations.

Companies or exhibitors are a useful source of income, sponsorship, prizes and potential speakers. If you put them in separate room, make sure that you put the refreshments in the same room; otherwise delegates may not take the time to visit them.

If you are using gift bags or delegate packs, do not make them too large or heavy. It can become a bit of juggling act, trying to carry everything.

Distributing parking, travel and accommodation information prior to the event is useful. On the day the Wi-Fi code is a must, we cannot cope without being connected these days. When it comes to lunch, even buffet style food can be hard to eat with flimsy plates and nowhere to sit, I understand why some events do not have seating at lunchtime, because they want to encourage us to move around the exhibitors and to network. I personally like having somewhere to sit and eat. For many SBMs, it is a treat to have a lunch break that is uninterrupted, without hearing the phrase, 'I know you are eating your lunch, but can I just ask you ...'

Delegates like having a choice of workshops. If you have any led by exhibitors, make sure it is not a hard sell for their product or service.

Location is important, wherever you choose people will choose not to come. I rarely go to events in London or the south because of the cost of travel. Many of the regional groups vary their location and hold joint events with other groups, to cover a wider area.

Even though local groups are growing in size and are able to host full day conference events in their own area, I would still encourage people to go to events further afield because you get to meet different people.

I think it is a nice touch to bring together those who are attending for the first time for a short welcome and introduction session.

View from an expert

Setting up an SBL group – Louise Hatswell FISBL, director of finance/business manager, Saint Pius X Catholic High School, Rawmarsh St Joseph's Catholic Primary School and Our Lady and St Joseph's Catholic Primary School

Working in the last maintained secondary school in my local authority became a very isolated role. Having attended the NASBM (now ISBL) National Conference and EdExec Live, I really valued the networking opportunities they provided. It made me realise that there were no opportunities like this available to me locally, so I decided I would look into setting up a local SBM group. After much research and contacting NASBM for advice, I had a very clear idea of the aims and vision for the group. The group would cover four local authorities and would welcome members from all phases and types of schools. I booked a room to hold an introductory meeting, prepared an agenda and presentation, and tentatively sent out email invitations. Within minutes my phone was ringing and my inbox was 'pinging' with people wanting to book a place at the meeting. All 50 places were booked and a waiting list set up within less than a week. The meeting went ahead with 57 delegates in attendance and another 20 who wanted to be involved with the group but couldn't attend on the day.

I made my presentation to the group, introducing myself, and explaining why I wanted to set up the group and what I hoped it would achieve. I gave each table a series of topics for discussion, such as potential membership fees, length and frequency of meetings, and whether to have sponsor involvement. I also asked for each table to list the key issues they felt SBMs faced at that time, and topics for keynote speakers or CPD workshops. The group overwhelmingly supported my suggestions, and when I asked if people would be prepared to join the group and pay the membership fee, the response was pretty much unanimously in favour.

So, a week later the South Yorkshire School Business Leadership Group was officially launched. The first year has been a whirlwind, the group now has over 155 members from across the four local authorities. We have a thriving online forum where members and sponsors have access to discussion boards to share good practice, ask for advice and obtain special offers or discounts. We have a GDPR working party within the group, creating resources and policies which will be shared with all members, and members are pairing up to audit each other to save costs.

We held our first annual conference, which was a great success and we co-hosted a conference with two other Yorkshire SBM groups. Our meetings are very much member driven, the agenda is informed by member evaluation and the CPD workshops are in direct response to member needs. We now have a committee in place, with each member being responsible for specific areas to share the workload.

We started our second year with all our members renewing their membership and most of our sponsors renewing their sponsorship, and many more joining us. We have negotiated many discounts and special offers for our members and we will be looking at areas where we can purchase collaboratively.

The feedback from our members has been overwhelmingly positive, and I have found it quite humbling to hear of the impact the group has had on some individuals, and in turn the children in their schools. After all, we are all working together for the same goal; to improve the life chances of the young people in our care.

Treat everyone as a potential coach

A good coach can change a game. A great coach can change a life.

John Wooden

Everyone you meet is a potential coach. You do not need to ask someone to be your coach, and they should not have to ask you to be theirs, you just need to ask the right questions. Start your power coaching questions with; what, how, who, where, when, why, which and describe. Discuss with your leadership team the potential to use coaching as a whole school model rather than as a strategy for addressing issues and underperformance.

Challenge and support for ultimate growth. This model shows where growth can happen. The ideal working culture for growth and continued improvement is through high challenge and high support. The impact of high challenge, low support is regression, whereby the employee retreats from the situation. The impact of low challenge, low support is stasis, little growth or improvement. The impact of high support, low challenge is confirmation and continuation of the norm.

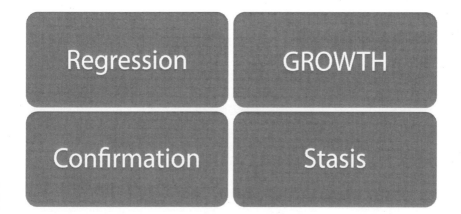

Next steps

Next time you go to a conference or a CPD event, think about one thing that you would like to improve. Ask as many people as you can; 'How do you do it?'

Top tip

Have lots of business cards to hand.

Achievements

> *We need to own our achievements rather than assuming our silent, hard work will be noticed. We need to get very loud. Be brave and do it. Be proud and celebrate it. Be loud and share it.*

WomenEd

Good leaders celebrate achievements and the best leaders know their staff well and understand who is comfortable with being recognised publicly and who prefers something quieter. There is a fine line between celebrating and appreciating achievements and being boastful. I think that as a group business managers and leaders are not very good at celebrating our own achievements. But if we want the raise the profile of the profession it is important that we share when we achieve a new qualification or an award, and what it means not only for us, but for the school as a whole.

I am proud to say that I am a fellow of ISBL, and I want to build awareness and understanding of what that actually means, by communicating what I have to achieve to meet the required specification. It involved demonstrating my capability against a number of areas, including my level of qualification, experience and leadership. To become a fellow, at the time of my application, there were stringent requirements:

- A level six or above qualification in a relevant discipline.
- At least three years of experience working at a senior level within the school business leadership profession.
- Demonstrate significant experience and evidence impact in at least two of the key professional standards areas, of which one had to be leading support services, the other areas were finance, procurement, HR, marketing and Infrastructure.
- Provide evidence of my commitment to CPD.
- Provide evidence of leadership and support within the profession.
- Demonstrate a high level of professional conduct.

Many business managers and leaders that I know are more qualified than most of their colleagues in schools, for example having undertaken Masters qualifications, a lot of which is done in their own time and for the main part self-funded. As I mentioned in my introduction, we have the power to change the story that we tell others and ourselves about our profession.

It is important that we document our personal progress and achievements. I keep a folder with examples of my work that I am proud of; systems and processes I have designed and implemented, templates that I have produced, certificates, thank you messages, articles and guest blogs, press releases and photos. They are all items that will pick me up on a bad day.

- Celebrate your own achievements.
- Celebrate your team's achievements.
- Celebrate and recognise the achievements of your peers.
- Be part of building recognition and understanding of our profession.
- Be the change.

Become a champion

Advocate for the people you work with, your school and importantly your pupils. Your place of work should be somewhere that you are proud to represent as a professional. Champion your school business professional peers and the work they do. Make connections and introduce your contacts to each other, either face-to-face or virtually, where you can see they would benefit from knowing each other. Making personal connections and building positive relationships can advance careers. Recommend people who have been great to work with, write them a testimonial that they can use in the future.

View from an expert

Looking for your next challenge? Why not become a specialist leader of education – Jo Marchant, AInsAM(Dip), Cert Acc, MBA, FISBL, school business leader

I am sitting in a taxi with two SBMs I have never met before going to the National Conference and we're chatting about our qualifications when one of them asks me, 'So what are you doing next?' That question encapsulates everything I love about our profession; the constant striving for personal improvement, the challenge and the opportunities that are open to all of us if we have the motivation and enthusiasm to grasp them.

In the first half of 2015, I was elected Chair of the Kent Association of Special Schools SBM Group and achieved NASBM (now ISBL) fellow status of which I am extremely proud. For my next challenge I was considering applying for the ADSBM course but felt that this was more aligned with moving to a large secondary academy and I wanted to remain within the special schools field. Talking with my deputy principal she told me about her experiences as a specialist leader of education (SLE) and that's what I decided my next challenge would be – to become an SLE.

So, what exactly is an SLE?

An SLE is an outstanding middle or senior leader with at least two years' leadership experience, expertise in a particular area (in my case school business management and financial management) and a successful track record of school improvement. SLEs are part of a strategy for developing leadership capacity in other schools using coaching and facilitation approaches to positively impact student outcomes. The aim is to ensure the sustainability of any implemented changes once an assignment has ended. SLEs are recruited by teaching schools to provide up to ten days of support a year to other schools as requested. The length of time required for an assignment inevitably depends upon its nature but could range from a two-day diagnostic exercise to a short-term full support role.

How do you become an SLE?

Firstly, you need to have the full support of your principal and a plan for how to cover your day job when out on SLE assignments. My principal was very supportive, and we agreed that increasing the finance officer's hours would allow me to fulfil an SLE role as well as providing some future-proofing for the school as we have a rising roll. The opportunity to apply to become an SLE came when my school and two other Kent special schools were awarded teaching school alliance status towards the end of 2015.

The application form must evidence that you meet certain criteria including what motivates you to participate in system leadership. One of the aspects of the education sector that has always impressed me is our willingness to share our knowledge with each other. I am a great believer in not re-inventing the wheel and imparting my knowledge and sharing my experience with others was something I wanted to expand on.

To evidence the significant impact of my contribution as a leader supporting leaders in other schools I cited the presentations that I give to the Kent Association of Special Schools SBM Group and the National Professional Qualification for Middle Leadership courses where I present on the Schools' Finance Value Standard (SFVS), value for money and developing an effective coach – participant relationship. For impact on my own school's performance I described a creative problem-solving workshop on absence management that I facilitated, the outcome of which resulted in decreased staff absence.

For the criteria of using coaching or facilitation skills to grow leadership in others leading to sustainable improvements, I focused on my coaching role for a teacher on the NPQML course in 2014/15 who was subsequently promoted to department head. For the last criteria of significantly challenging, collaborating, motivating and/or inspiring colleagues to establish new and innovative working practices, I described the budget focus group that I set up following a discussion at my local authority's Schools' Funding Forum. This involved six SBMs collaborating with the local authority's schools budget team to identify and improve budget-building best practice for special schools, the results of which were disseminated to all 24 special schools in Kent. Finally, my principal had to write a detailed statement against set criteria evidencing my abilities and achievements.

Shortly after applying I was invited to participate in an assessment process consisting of a ten-minute presentation and an interview by a panel of four headteachers from different teaching schools including the one I was applying to. My preparation for the assessment included speaking with an SBM SLE to get more information about the role, reading about other SBMs' SLE experiences online and preparing answers to likely interview questions. I took a logical approach to the presentation focusing on the role of the SLE, how my qualifications, skills and current roles supported my areas of expertise, how my experience to date had prepared me for the SLE role, and how I could maximise my impact as an SLE. I used a small number of impactful slides to get my points across.

The interview panel make their recommendation regarding appointments which then had to be ratified. I was very excited to learn that I had passed the selection process. There is compulsory core training, following which I will be an accredited SLE ready for deployment. It is at that point that the teaching school alliance can advertise the SLE availability on their website.

My next challenge will be my first assignment, what is yours going to be?

Elevator pitch

When you are asked the question 'So, what do you do?' how often have you waffled and gone in to a long explanation about what a school business manager does? I do it all the time, rattling off all the areas I am responsible for and trying to convey what part I play in the school leadership. So my short answer tends to be 'I deal with finance and things like that'.

Say you are at a conference and you can see the CEO of the trust that you dream of working at. You know that this individual is forward thinking, outward looking, innovative, receptive to the ideas of others and greatly values the business management part of the organisation. This person values people above all else. You know you would make the perfect team. You know a little bit about them and read an interesting press release about their latest project, which is your perfect conversation starter. However, how are you going to let them know who you are and what you can do? It is all down to how you introduce yourself.

You need an elevator pitch that is short, concise and to the point. Aim for 20-30 seconds long, and about 150 words and highlight why you are valuable. What project could you talk about, that they might be interested in? Remember to let your personality come through. If you can, swap business cards and follow up your introduction with an email.

Embrace social media

> *Social tools are not just about giving people a voice, but giving them a way to collaborate, contribute and connect.*

John Stepper

There is a growing community of school business professionals from a variety of roles and backgrounds using social media platforms including Twitter, LinkedIn and Facebook to communicate, network and collaborate with colleagues and stakeholders all over the world.

You can use social media to share your ideas and views; and discuss them with other school business professionals. Use it as a research tool. You can ask for support by messaging someone directly or publishing an open post, and even post questionnaires or polls. Utilise it to ask questions and learn new things. Create your own professional learning and support network.

You can stay up to date with the latest education sector stories and information and debate whether they are going to help or hinder you. It is always useful to get other people's perspective on something. And don't forget to market your organisation through your professional profile.

Using social media has helped me to find a group of like-minded school business professionals who are innovative and forward thinking. It gives you access to professionals who you would otherwise never meet.

Take on the Twitter challenge:

- Create an account.
- Connect with other school business leaders.
- Follow ten accounts.
- Quote a tweet and give your opinion on it.
- Retweet a tweet that you find interesting.
- Join in with Twitter chats.

Important note

Remember to check your school's policy on using social media, and your security settings. Adhere to the usual confidentiality expectations. Remember that even if you state that the views expressed are purely personal, they will also reflect your organisation in the eyes of other users.

Impact

You cannot get through a single day without having an impact on the world around you. What you do makes a difference, and you have to decide what kind of difference you want to make.

Jane Goodall

Strive for progress not perfection

I learned an important business leadership lesson from an inspiring woman that I worked for in an accountancy practice. Her name is Jacqueline Cole and she taught me about perspective.

When I worked for her I was preparing statutory accounts and returns. One day I was working on a sales account reconciliation and I had got a balance with a small difference of a few pounds. As an accountant, I was getting frustrated that it did not balance exactly. I checked the opening debtor, I ticked and checked that all the sales invoices and credit notes for the period were listed, I checked the receipts, and I checked that the closing balance agreed to the invoices not paid. Still it did not balance, and I could not spot why.

I went to talk to Jackie and asked her what I should do. She asked me if I had checked all the balances and I confirmed that I had. She looked over what I had done, and her reply was that it was fine, I did not need to do anything further. That was not the answer I was expecting. I asked her to explain her response and she told me that it was clear that I had done a thorough job, but there was not any value to be gained from me spending more time looking for the difference. Doing the same thing repeatedly, trying to get a different outcome was a waste of my time and therefore her money. Putting it in to perspective, a few pounds was immaterial. It taught me an important lesson about valuing time, spending it fruitfully and keeping things in perspective.

Focus on progress and excellence, not perfection. Work smarter not harder, because if you keep doing the same things in the same way, nothing is going to change, and nothing is going to improve.

Delegation

Learn to delegate effectively. If you do not like delegating, you need to examine and understand why that is. Is it because you are a perfectionist? You do not trust anyone to do it as well as you can? You want it done right now? Or is the real reason because you have not had time to show someone else how to do the task? Doing this may take more time the first time the person does it, but it will save you time in the long run.

That is not to say that you should abdicate responsibility, you should still be aware of what is happening in your team. Here are a number of ways in which you can monitor progress:

- Tracking documents
- Daily or weekly team meetings
- Task logging system
- One to one meetings
- Performance management
- Audit reports

Having an open door policy and being approachable has always been important to me, allowing and encouraging staff to raise issues and concerns. If staff are holding back on being open and honest, they are not going to be focused on progress and improvement.

But you do not want a queue of staff outside the door every morning, and you can avoid this by giving them a regular voice and platforms to share their views. It should be an expectation of all managers to behave and lead their teams in the same way, ensuring that they listen, communicate and respond.

Reflection

The purpose of reflection is to consider your response to experiences, events, new information, thoughts and feelings. Many leadership qualifications include it as part of the course or qualification. Delegates are required to keep a reflective log, it is an important part of continuous learning.

How do I be reflective?

I believe it comes from practice and the more you do it, the easier it becomes. Build it in to all your learning practices such as training courses, performance management, and analysing personal performance in specific situations.

Have a structure and make it a habit, book in a regular daily or weekly time slot that is set aside to reflect on the events from the day or week, and keep a separate diary or journal. I try to do a weekly reflection and I write down an experience or an event as I recall it. By writing it down, I am aiming to get at the important details behind what I was disappointed or annoyed with, to enable me to go back to the issue or respond to it differently next time. If a situation escalated, why did it happen? Did the person not feel listened to? Did I not understand what their main concern was? After reflecting on my challenges, I always end with writing about the positive things that have happened.

Self-assess and evaluate. Consider advice that you are given from others. As a leader, just because you are given advice does not mean you have to act on it, you need to decide what will work for you. Give yourself advice on how to do things differently or better next time, developing your practice and learning from your experience.

As a leader, it is vital to learn to shut out the noise and the chatter, to enable you to focus on what is important.

Impact

This is the most important piece advice that I want to share with you. This is the one thing I want you to remember from reading this book. It has become my mantra and my reason for doing what I do and reasoning how I spend my time:

If what you are doing isn't having a positive impact on pupil outcomes, why are you doing it?

The reason that I have been passionate about writing this book is that I remember vividly the amount that I have had to learn to get to my current position and level of understanding. Many people along the way have supported me and I wanted to share what I have learned, in the hope that it makes the working lives of others a little bit easier and to show you that there is a wealth of experience out there that you can access if you make the time to be an outward looking leader.

It was important to me to share the experiences from other school business professionals because everyone knows something that someone else does not know. Particular areas of knowledge and skills can be learned, but experience gives an understanding that goes deeper.

If there is something that you want to do, and you feel the something is holding you back, whether it be professionally or personally, then you need to turn that barrier in to a goal for you to achieve and overcome.

When I was a teenager going to university was not an option for me, there was no way that we could afford it. I was determined that my lack of a degree was not going to hold me back; I just needed to find another way. It was a longer way, but it got me to the same place that I wanted to be. I found an employer who took me on as an accounts assistant and supported me to do my Association of Accounting Technicians (AAT) qualification. I really enjoyed the accounting side and I decided to take the next step.

I drafted a letter and my CV, printed them on good quality paper, and then sent them to ten local accountancy companies. I explained that I was keen to move in to the sector and to do training. From those ten letters I had two prompt responses, with invitations to interview and both offered me a job; there was a £500 difference in the salary offer and 30 miles between the two companies. Both offers meant taking a pay cut, but it was sacrifice I was willing to take at that stage of my career because I was sure it would lead to a better future. I ended up taking the lower offer, because it meant that my husband and I could be nearer our families.

Two other companies which had kept my details on file asked if I was still looking for an opportunity, which was encouraging. I had not waited for something to happen to me, I had gone out and made it happen for myself. I know this way of recruiting is not the way we generally do it in the education sector, but there is nothing stopping you from approaching an employer you want to work for and asking them to keep you in mind should a vacancy come up in the future.

I got my Association of Chartered Certified Accountants (ACCA) qualification the hard way. I was three months pregnant when I took my final exam and experiencing horrendous waves of nausea most of the time although I think the nerves overcame the nausea for the duration of the exam. I funded some of it myself, having tuition in the evenings and getting the train for an hour there and back to Birmingham to attend courses on Saturdays and Sundays. Nevertheless, the effort and cost were worth it. Getting that qualification meant a huge amount to me, and I know that my family, particularly my parents are proud of me.

It is funny seeing my daughters now; they have the same gritty determination that I have. My Dad looks at them, watching me tell them to be careful and he tells me that I would never listen to anyone who told me I could not do something either, and smiles.

We all have a past. We all have a story to tell. We all have the same number of hours in a day, and various demands on our time. Manage your time, do not let it manage you. If something is not working, change it.

We all make an impact. There may be an element of luck when it comes to being in the right place at the right time. But those opportunities, the really good ones, may be more likely to appear if you put yourself in the right place at the right time. As one inspirational leader told me, when it comes to potential employers you need to fill their space in some way, whether it be at a networking event or on social media. Make yourself known to them, so when they see your name on an application form, their first thought is that they need to see you at interview. It is not about being part of some old boys' club, getting a job with a nod and wink, it is about being recognised and appreciated for being the professional you already are, and creating the opportunity to demonstrate what you can do and what impact you can make.

I will take you back to the list from the beginning of the book, of things that school business professionals said will make the most difference to pupils:

- Building relationships with local businesses
- Reviewing every process
- Devising a creative PPA plan
- Creating a bank of resources
- Developing a summer school provision
- Income generation
- Making links with the local community

What would your list include?

Geoff Barton, ASCL General Secretary, highlighted at the 2018 ASCL Conference that the main issues affecting school leaders are:

- Funding
- Recruitment and retention
- Workload
- Accountability
- Ethical leadership
- Young people's mental health

If these are the biggest challenges and the things that will make the greatest difference, then it is our duty to take action and make the time to focus on these priorities. You have the power to make the change. You can make the difference to the learning and development opportunities that are available to the young people in your care. Leadership is all about raising the aspirations of others and encouraging them to achieve outcomes that they would not have thought possible. Empower people to be better, through the words you choose to use and the actions you decide to take. Leadership is somewhat akin to thinking and acting like a goose. When geese fly in formation they communicate constantly, and when the one at the front gets tired, they swap places. If they drift off alone out of the V formation, they feel the wind more, have to work harder to keep up, and move back. When one is injured, they will protect their own. It seems as though there is mutual respect among the team.

We are a team, we can ask for help when we need it and we can offer it to others. We can all be facilitators instead of obstacles. You are the link that can join up teaching and learning with strategic business leadership. You need to lead yourself well before you try to lead others. Senior leaders and colleagues can champion your work, but ultimately you are the greatest champion for business leadership in your school, organisation, community, network and beyond.

Once you have identified the areas that you want to focus on, test your choices with the following question in everything that you do; 'What impact will it make?'

Processes and procedures take up a lot of time, so constant re-appraisal of them to ensure that they are fit for purpose and running with as little wastage as possible is vital. Ask yourself what you can remove, replace or improve to ensure the most efficient and effective impact. Embrace technology and explore how it can be harnessed to have the greatest impact and create sustainable development.

People are our greatest resource and it is part of our role to get them on board and invested in delivering the organisation's vision to ensure the best possible outcomes and impact for pupils. To sell that vision you must be clear on those expected outcomes and methods for achieving them. Collaboration expands the expertise and resources available, we cannot do everything ourselves, and the role can become isolated and lonely without colleagues and peers being there to support us. It works both ways, we need others to support us and we have lots to offer in supporting others. Think about how you can help others to have an impact, and how others can help you.

Think about vision. Not just the school's or MAT's vision. What is your vision? Does it match or complement that of the organisation? Are you focused on impact? What is holding you back? Others can only hold us back if we let them.

Think about ethical leadership. Ask yourself 'Am I doing the right thing?' Lead with trust, honesty, objectivity and skill. Be resilient, challenge even when faced with resistance, be committed to the pupils, collaborate, utilise your personal drive, stay aware and be reflective. We cannot get it right every time, but we can try to do better next time and learn from our mistakes. Always act with integrity and respect for others. Fundamentally, if it does not feel right, if it is not sitting well with you, do not accept it, revisit the issue and find another way.

So, what is next for you?

Who knows, but I hope that reading this book will have given you some ideas and inspiration. Perhaps this checklist could be a start:

- Have a clear understanding of your skills, experience and qualifications.
- Understand by self-auditing where you currently sit in the education leadership landscape and where you want to be.
- Be assertive and confident that you are a highly skilled and experienced professional.

- Be prepared to invest your time and yourself in professional development opportunities. Broaden your network and understanding and stretch beyond your limits. Ensure that you consider changing your context before changing from the profession you love.

- Draw your own map and decide which pathways you will take, you do not have to follow others' directions.

- Demonstrate your impact.

The future

The best way to predict the future is to create it.

Abraham Lincoln (attrib.)

For school business leaders of the future, I see analytical insights as being important, and the embracing of technology and innovation to provide creative ways to deliver outstanding services. Harnessing technology has transformed our lives over time; we live very differently to our parents and grandparents. Innovations and new products will only develop quicker and further and become more and more sophisticated, changing the ways we can learn, live and work. If we do not keep up with technology, learning and growing alongside it, then we will surely be left behind.

A special education centre in Poole won a national award last year for 'Digital innovation/ed-tech school of the year'. They have embraced technology to help their students, who have physical disabilities and complex health needs, to access and engage with the curriculum. The pupils use mobile devices, advanced electronics for auditory feedback, gesture-controlled motion and eye-sensing technology, to help them develop their motor skills and to explore and affect their environment. This type of innovation and forward thinking has the ability to transform a pupil's experiences and make what previously seemed impossible, possible. This is life changing work and as school business leaders we have a critical part to play in making these projects possible.

Another school has been recognised for the 'Best use of technology' for the innovative centre they have created and now staff throughout the day. It includes a robotics lab, a virtual reality room, a green screen and editing room, animation pods, a video conferencing room and a drone that films in HD. These are the sorts of resources that most schools can only dream of having, because they are shackled by dealing with the pressures that are in the here and now; funding issues, teacher workload and recruitment challenges are the norm in many schools and MATs.

If there were no limits and no financial constraints, just a blank piece of paper for my ideal design, I would create education hubs. Each hub would be a mixed-use site, with indoor and outdoor learning spaces, co-located health and welfare services, provision for three meals a day, amazing sensory and calm spaces and support all year round for all pupils. They would be environments that would support every child to succeed.

We need to use all the data at our disposal effectively to forecast, inform our planning and manage risk, particularly concerning financial planning. We must learn and build the skills to be strategic decision-makers and develop commercial awareness, embracing the need to take calculated risks. Cyber security is an excellent example of a key area in which to keep your knowledge and practice current; as methods to secure information improve, so too does the sophistication of the strategies that criminals employ.

Keep up to date with how your whole school or MAT works and try to identify and decipher patterns. Be aware of the developments and trends set by the large academy chains who have the power and influence to make changes which can potentially affect the sector locally and nationally.

There will never be less to do in our working day, so continue to hone your ability to choose between competing priorities. Increase your business acumen through understanding what drives the business, evaluating growth, monitoring what works and what does not, and delivering continuous improvement. Be skilled in the ability to visualise numbers and predict their impact. Be the person who flags up early warning signs, reports potential issues and presents solutions. Prioritise your own wellbeing and manage your time so that you have the energy and capacity – physically, mentally and emotionally to be efficient, effective and innovative.

Develop leadership and communication skills and build resilient, fast and reliable teams which deliver efficient services and accurate information for strategic decision-making. Retain and develop your staff by being forward thinking and encouraging CPD and progression. Put wellbeing at the heart and soul of your organisation, and ensure that staff have the appropriate balance of stretch, encouragement, training and downtime. Endow them with strategies to help manage the 24/7 lifestyles we have created. Ensure that we are creating and developing workplaces where children and adults alike want to be, by making them as exciting and stimulating as possible. They should be learning environments which foster strong work and team ethics, where we check in with people to see if they are OK, and where we are always supportive and encouraging. Remember that feeling as a child when you woke up early and jumped out of bed because something exciting was happening that day? We need to bottle that feeling and release it in to our schools, breathing life and purpose in to our organisations.

The closing words are from the brilliant Val Andrew, who is the previous ASCL Business Leadership Specialist.

Use her words to reflect on your future in school business management and leadership and choose the direction you will take...

What does the future look like for the 'next generation' school business leader? How do I prepare myself to be a viable part of that future vision for the profession?

This book successfully pulls together a plethora of advice, guidance, reference to a range of tried and tested tools, techniques, resources and not least the shared and candid experiences of practising school business leaders. To have all this information in one place will undoubtedly prove to be an invaluable resource for many.

The current challenging fiscal climate has brought the SBL profession into much sharper focus than ever before. We are the group of school leaders with the necessary skills to navigate budget pressures, to deliver the optimum model of efficiency and effectiveness, to seek out savings in areas previously overlooked, and last but by no means least we share that sector wide commitment to ensuring that the young people in our schools, colleges and academies get the best possible deal in terms of the education they deserve. It has become obvious to all (some are later to that party than others!) that as a profession school business leaders are the link between best possible value and efficient, effective models of operation throughout each individual organisation. We understand the imperative for a lack of orthodoxy in our approach, and the need to probe and ask difficult questions about everything that has a cost attached to it.

Incredibly, there remain a few pockets of resistance to the integral nature of the SBL role and some practitioners continue to experience a serious lack of recognition for their endeavours. The outdated concept that anyone with a 'business' focus cannot realistically have an impact on the educational outcomes of pupils and students is still evident in some places. I know that the notion that commerciality has no place in a state run education system is still held dear by some and this book has some good advice for those unfortunate practitioners who are on the receiving end of such behaviours. The reality is that at every level within our sector there is a growing appreciation of the benefits of clear and co-ordinated links between education and the business communities across the land. Paul Drechsler, CEO of the CBI, addressed the ASCL Annual Conference in March and articulated the importance of greater collaboration between the business community and education. This will support the development of the necessary skills young people require that are more closely tailored to employment opportunities of the future, but it will also reinforce the concept that there needs to be more of a professional and business dynamic across educational leadership in order for our schools, academies and colleges to be sustainable.

So what does this brave new world hold for our profession and how can we prepare to be a part of that next generation of school business leaders?

It is clear that the system itself continues to evolve and along with it the SBL profession.

The settings

There will be opportunities in single educational settings (I firmly believe that some standalone schools have the potential to survive longer term) albeit fewer than before where a generalist type role will be most appropriate. The advent of more school groups – be those MATs or federations – will inevitably lead to a degree of specialisation and ultimately an increasing number of executive level roles, with some practitioners aspiring to the CEO role within a group setting.

SBL practitioners who have career aspirations to serve within executive structures will need to be more mobile and prepared to expand their skills and competencies appropriately. ASCL's guidance paper 'Effective Business Functionality within developing MATs' sets out some clear principles and case studies to demonstrate how some organisations have rolled out staffing structures to deliver a range of business functions and to accommodate issues arising from growth. Looking at the case studies available, it is obvious that there is no 'one model' solution that will fit every scenario. So, what we will see is variation and potentially the scope for practitioners to be mobile within a MAT setting to broaden SBL experiences.

Skills

Skills and competencies required by the next generation SBL will need to be varied and a mix of technical and strategic in focus. Depending on the setting, it may be that some practitioners will need to pursue the specialist route and acquire recognised qualifications (accountancy, HR, marketing, estates management *etc.*) in order to discharge their duties effectively, whilst others may opt for the SBM Qualifications Programme – a route accredited by the ILM (Institute for Leadership and Management) and familiar to most as the updated versions of CSBM, DSBM, ADSBM *etc*.

A robust commitment to a programme of ongoing CPD will be essential for next generation SBLs. Being proactive and seeking out opportunities to develop new skills in anticipation of a need at school will be advantageous. For example, within the growing MATs, new roles may be required such as:

- Marketing and brand management across a group
- Contracts management for managed services
- Procurement co-ordination
- Compliance and statutory management
- Income generation and fundraising
- Multi-faceted estates and infrastructure management

Not a definitive list – new aspects of business functionality are emerging all the time.

Alongside the above it will also be key to continue to develop leadership skills – ASCL are committed to advocating ethical leadership. Geoff Barton, ASCL General Secretary, mentions this earlier. It is good to use a values-based approach when making leadership (or any professional) decisions *ie*:

- The sleeping test – if I do this will I sleep at night?
- The newspaper test – would I do this if it was reported in the papers?
- The mirror test – if I do this will I be able to look myself in the mirror?
- The teenager test – would I mind my children knowing I was doing this?

(Taken from leadershipmatters.org.uk)

Collaboration, networking and sharing best practice

This book is a great example of this in practice.

Opportunities for networking and collaborating are increasing for the SBL profession. There are more regional groups now than ever before and whilst there remain some 'barren' areas there has been a proactivity on the part of the DfE to support the development of more regional groups and hubs. It is also essential to engage in national events to ensure that the wider context/challenge is fully understood and strategised. I'd be keen to see the development of one national conference for the profession to raise the profile even further.

Isolation within the role has already been mentioned in this book – the networks can help combat this and guard against being overwhelmed so make sure you are a member of one. With the advances of technology and social media the barriers to engagement with other SBL professionals should decrease – but be wary about the 'rules of engagement' as none of us are immune from the darker side of these communication channels!

Be resilient

Probably one of the hardest things to achieve – my input earlier in the book refers to the necessary agility we need as professionals working in challenging circumstances. Being resilient helps us to maintain our responsiveness and helps us to perform when under pressure. Some useful ways we can help develop and build our own levels of resilience include:

- Maintaining good relationships – both at home and at work
- Accepting the things we cannot change
- Embracing self-reflection – one of the hardest things to commit to
- Retain a longer term perspective
- Work on your own self-confidence
- Take care of your own personal health and well-being

And finally...

The main issues as highlighted by Geoff Barton, which are facing all school leaders, were highlighted earlier on in this book:

- Funding
- Recruitment and retention
- Workload
- Accountability
- Ethical leadership
- Young people's mental health

There is no doubt we are all motivated with the best of intentions – we are certainly not in this job for the money! It goes without saying that we have to demonstrate our own value within the leadership function and be mindful of the actual impact we have as professionals working within the sector. We can and do have a direct impact on all of the above but need to be part of a high performing team to have half a chance of solving all those problems at local level. Most importantly what we do actually does impact on the life chances of the young people in the system today.

It is probably relevant here to quote the story of the NASA janitor who when questioned by the President of the United States about his role, responded that he was helping to put a man on the moon!

To preserve your position as a next generation SBL, make sure you sort out your own insurance policy and join a leadership union!

Appendix

ASCL Guidance papers

(Available from www.ascl.org.uk/help-and-advice/guidance-papers/)

Pensions and Tax Liability
May 2018

Setting Pay for Executive Heads/Principals and Chief Executive Officers
November 2017

Changes to Ofsted Section 5 and Section 8 Handbooks for 2017
October 2017

Effective Business Functionality within Developing MATs
September 2017

International School Exchanges and Visits: Homestays
March 2019

Understanding and Interpreting the 2017 Key Stage 2 Results
September 2017

Area Based Reviews
November 2018

A Levels, AS Levels and GCSEs 2018: Requesting reviews of marking and making appeals
May 2018

Marking and Feedback
September 2018

Lesson Planning and Teacher Resources
July 2017

Phonics: a guide to teaching reading in schools
July 2017

How to build effective home-school partnerships - joint guidance with ASCL, PTA UK and NAHT
July 2017

What governing boards should expect from school leaders, and what school leaders should expect from governing boards - joint guidance with LGA, NAHT and NGA
June 2017

Social Networking, Social Media and Email: protecting your professional reputation
July 2018

Engaging with your MP:
getting involved in the policy making process
May 2017

Mathematics Teaching for Mastery
May 2017

Using the Headteacher Standards
April 2017

Due Dilligence and Risk Management
May 2018

Strategic Finance: design principles and financial reporting
February 2017

Inspection, SIMS and the Single Central Record
October 2019

Understanding and Interpreting the 2016 Key Stage 2 Results
January 2017

Setting Pay for School Business Leaders and School Business Managers – Under review at the time of publishing
May 2018

Income Generation
May 2018

Effective Procurement
May 2018

Statutory Duties Relating to Safety, Safeguarding and Radicalisation
Revised October 2016

An Exploratory Evaluation Framework: safety, safeguarding and radicalisation
Revised June 2016

Summary of the Special Educational Needs (SEN) Code of Practice 2015
April 2016

Progression and Assessment in History: short-form guidance
February 2016

Framework Supporting Progression and Assessment in History
February 2016

Progression and Assessment in History
January 2016

Teacher Quality, Standards and Appraisal
December 2015

Leadership of Strategic Improvement Planning and Self-evaluation
June 2018

Leadership of Professional Development and Learning

September 2018

Summary of the Key Changes to the School Teachers Pay and Conditions Document 2015 and 2014

September 2015

School Teachers' Pay 2015-16

July 2015

Taking the Next Step – Considering joining or forming a group of schools

June 2019

Taking the Next Step – Joining a Multi-Academy Trust

June 2019

Taking the Next Step – Forming a Multi-Academy Trust

June 2019

Making your PFI contact work for you

January 2019

The Baker Clause

November 2019

#BeTheChange